The Way It Was

GW00536973

The Way It Was

A History of the Oxfordshire Cotswolds in Old Photographic Postcards

Derek James Bason
Gregory Lee Bason

The Breedon Books
Publishing Company
Derby

First published in Great Britain by
The Breedon Books Publishing Company Limited
Breedon House, 44 Friar Gate, Derby, DE1 1DA.
2000

Map on page 11 courtesy of the Bodleian Library, University of Oxford.
C17: (63) OS ¼, sheet 8.

ISBN 1 85983 189 3

Printed and bound by Butler & Tanner Ltd., Selwood Printing Works,
Caxton Road, Frome, Somerset.

Colour separations and jacket printing by
GreenShires Group Ltd., Leicester.

For my father, Derek James Bason

Acknowledgements

My father's love of local history and collecting old postcards and photographs resulted in the original idea for *The Way It Was* in the early 1980s.

Following my father's death in 1986, *The Way It Was* lay unfinished for many years until, in January 1998, I determined to complete his work. At that time it consisted of about 60 postcards arranged into six chapters. Over the last two years I have added around 50 postcards and captions, while keeping the overall structure of the book the same.

Over the years many people and organisations, both local and national, have contributed towards *The Way It Was*. Museums, libraries, local people, friends, and family have supplied valuable information, kindly lent postcards, and shared their memories. Without their help this book would not have been possible. But my greatest thanks go to my sister for her thoughtful suggestions and patient proofreading, and to my mother and my fiancée for their support and encouragement.

Contents

Introduction

T HE 20TH CENTURY saw some of the most dramatic changes in the history of humankind. We moved from an age when the letter and postcard were the only means of keeping in touch, to an age when people regularly communicated with each other all over the world via telephones, computers, and satellites. The century began with the bicycle, horse, and steam locomotive as the main methods of transport, and ended in an era of private car ownership and relatively inexpensive international travel. The nature of work also continued to change as traditional manufacturing declined and agriculture responded to a more competitive and global marketplace. This shift towards employment in the service industries, and tourism in particular, is sure to continue in the 21st century. Many traditional rural recreations and pastimes have disappeared or been adapted for modern times. New leisure pursuits have arisen that would have been impossible to imagine when our grandparents were young.

There can be no doubt that, since the turn of the last century, English life has changed forever. The quiet, unhurried, and more communal way of life depicted by the postcards in this book has all but disappeared. The village itself no longer exists in glorious isolation, and our towns are noisier, less gentle, and less distinct in personality. However, while possibly lamenting such changes, we should be wary of wishing to return to the 'good old days', for then there was much hardship and fewer opportunities. Advances in health, education, and technology have led to greatly increased levels of personal freedom and opportunity, and I ask the reader to bear this in mind as they read this book.

The geographical region covered by *The Way It Was* could loosely be described as the Oxfordshire Cotswolds and surrounding area. That is, the region from Banbury in the north to Witney in the south, and from Middleton Stoney in the east to the border with Gloucestershire and Warwickshire in the west. Although Oxfordshire was not intended to be a distinct unit when its borders were laid out in about 1010, the area covered by this book has always been characterised and influenced by the Cotswold Hills, which in places rise to over 700 feet. The hills are good for sheep grazing, and in the Middle Ages the Cotswold wool trade brought much wealth to the towns of Witney, Burford, and Chipping Norton.

The towns and villages in this region contain many fine buildings that bear witness to an opulent past. The characteristic building material in this area is grey limestone and Stonesfield slate. In the north of the county, in the neighbourhood of Banbury, the limestone changes to a golden-brown colour due to iron deposits. It is from this ironstone that many pretty villages were built; Wroxton, Bloxham, Horley, and Hornton are but a few examples.

The Way It Was primarily covers the period from the turn of the century to the eve of World War Two, with some references to earlier and later times. Although not presented in chronological order, the book takes us from the Edwardian Golden Age, through the horrors of World War One, and on to the dramatic changes of the 1920s and 1930s. It is the effects of the Great War and the rapid advances in transportation and communications that make this period of our social history such an interesting area for study.

I hope that this pictorial social history of north-west Oxfordshire will attract readers of all ages. The eldest will be reminded of people, places, and events from their childhood, while the youngest can learn a little about the world of their parents or grandparents. Whatever their age, it is surely with fascination and perhaps with a little foreboding that they will consider how everyday life may change in the first 100 years of the new millennium.

Gregory Lee Bason
Long Hanborough, Oxfordshire.
January 2000

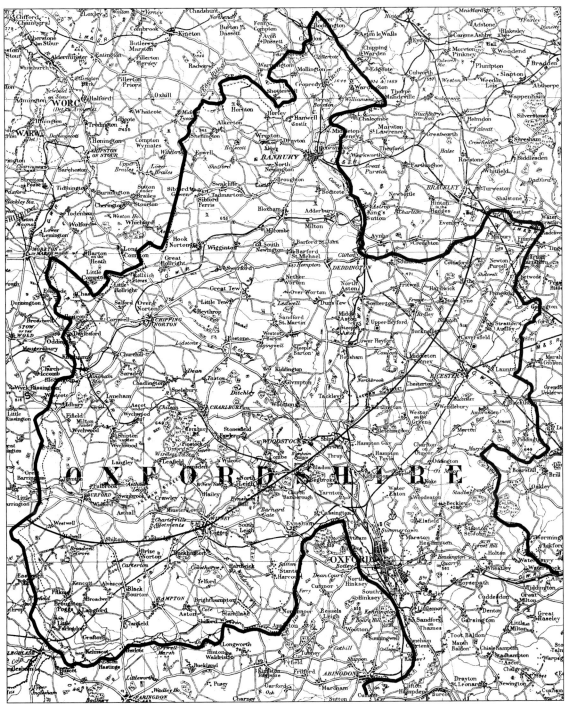

A map of central and north Oxfordshire, showing the county border prior to the county boundary changes of 1974. The area covered by this book lies north of the thin black line that runs across the centre of the county.

Chapter One
The Rural Scene

Cropredy. A sunny day as a horse and cart slowly makes its way up the lane to Williamscot in the mid 1920s. Cropredy is one of the most northern villages in the county. The Church of St Mary, built in 1320, houses a suit of armour discovered on the site of the Battle of Cropredy Bridge, which took place in 1644 during the Civil War.

Burdrop. A typical small Oxfordshire village as it was in 1910. The sender, who wrote the postcard on 22 July 1910, says: 'Here it is stormy, warm, cold, hot, windy, wet, brilliant sunshine, etc. etc., all in a day, most trying for haymaking.'

Barford St Michael. A quiet corner, yet a village full of life. Typically, on May Day the children would go around the village looking very gay and bright, bedecked with flowers and carrying Union Jacks. Cricket matches and fireworks often featured in May Day celebrations.

Thatched cottages, Milcombe. The doorways to these mellowed stone and thatched cottages are reached by walking up the narrow brick path, past a border of typical cottage garden flowers. Notice the wood leaning against a shed, drying out ready for the open fire.

Ploughing match. These matches were a regular feature in the agricultural calendar, so much so that some ploughmen had a match plough that was only used at these events. A single plough pulled by two horses is pictured here; a double plough would have used three horses.

Minster Lovell. A tranquil street scene photographed before the arrival of the telephone and television. A channel runs alongside the road helping to guide rainwater into the nearby River Windrush during wet weather. Wooden bridges providing accesss to the enchanting cottages complete this delightful scene.

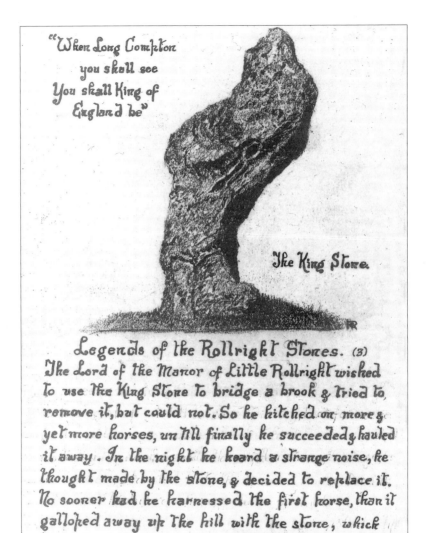

"When Long Compton
you shall see
You shall King of
England be"

The King Stone.

Legends of the Rollright Stones. (3)
The Lord of the Manor of Little Rollright wished
to use The King Stone to bridge a brook & tried to
remove it, but could not. So he hitched on more &
yet more horses, un till finally he succeeded & hauled
it away. In the night he heard a strange noise, he
thought made by the stone, & decided to replace it.
No sooner had he harnessed the first horse, than it
galloped away up the hill with the stone, which
leapt immediately into its old position.

Rollright Stones. These stones have been part of the Oxfordshire landscape for thousands of years. Generations treading the path around the stone circle have wondered at the four stones called the Whispering Knights. Sometimes overlooked, but equally part of this ancient scene, is the solitary King's Stone, 100 paces north of the circle. It stands some eight feet tall on a 700 foot high ridge.

Middleton Stoney. A rural village that looks deceptively deserted, but in fact was a place of daylong activity. Early morning would see domestic servants and gardeners hurrying to Middleton Park, and boys from the age of 13 setting out to do a day's work on the farm. The older folk would be making rugs, sawing wood, fetching water, and making jam, yet still finding time to tend the garden.

The Grange Gardens, Ascott-under-Wychwood.
A peaceful retreat. The sender of this card agrees as
she writes, 'We are here for the rest cure, it is a treat
to do just as we like but the time will go too quickly.'
Posted at Ascott-under-Wychwood on 16 July 1913.

Fritwell. This rural farm scene of unmade roads, iron railings, and chickens free to roam was photographed sometime before 1913, when the first autumn leaves were beginning to fall.

The vegetable garden. This photograph was taken during an era when you went without if you did not grow it yourself. It was hard to find the money for seeds and plants, and seed was always kept from the previous year's harvest. To actually buy a 'score' of plants was very rare. A well-stocked garden was essential, and while country folk might not have been educated, they were rich in the knowledge of soil, weather, and accurate planting times. It took experience and skill to produce food from a garden every week throughout the year.

Salford. This superb old photograph was taken in 1908. It gives an insight into working-class folk; characters of a bygone age. This was a village gathering, a time to join together in sharing a social life, but the photograph clearly captures the individuality of the club members.

Sunday stroll. This young lad in his 'Sunday best' was probably out for a Sunday evening stroll with his parents when this photograph was taken. It shows him in a wheat field, in front of a 'stook' of corn (the name given to a method of stacking for drying). 'I want it well cut! Well bound! Well shocked!', would have been the traditional cry. A figure was sometimes made from twisted sheaves of the last corn to be cut. This was hung up and kept for good luck until the next year's harvest.

Hook Norton. Nature looks its best in the countryside, but when the elements are against you the effects can be quite dramatic. The villagers of Hook Norton discovered this when they woke up on Sunday, 22 September 1935 after the great hailstorm.

Cornwell, or Cornewelle as it was spelt in the *Domesday Book.* A village with a matured, rustic look with its established gardens enclosed by drystone walling, and cottage roofs either thatched, or clad in Stonesfield tiles.

Wroxton. Lord North and the Abbey have long been associated with Wroxton, so much so that this pretty, rural village, a community in its own right, could be overlooked. Careful study of the photograph shows the village post office and sundial next door to the forge, with its blacksmith in his leather apron. There are village folk in the street as well as a farmyard horse and cart and various animals. All these complete a scene of truly yesteryear.

Chapter Two
Somewhere to Live

Sibford Ferris. The village post office was also the family home. On the death of a village postmaster or postmistress the location of the post office moved to the home of the new village official.

Tadmarton. Tiny, newly thatched cottages with bread ovens, built of local stone. These were very often home to large families, mainly employed as labourers in agriculture or as domestic servants.

The Litchfield Arms, Enstone. This imposing old inn must have been home for many families over the years, but they may not all have lived at the Litchfield Arms since old inns had a habit of changing their signs. In the early 1800s, a change to a name including the word 'Arms' was quite common, but a really old inn would have been called the Fox or the Star. A picture sign would tell its name; after all it was for the benefit of a generation of people of whom very few could read.

'A bit of old Charlbury'. This photograph shows Armada Cottage and the Old Talbot in Thames Street. These two cottages, built from coursed rubble with stone slate roofs, were probably built as a single house. A plaque outside Armada Cottage dates the building from 1587. The Greyhound, or Dog, became known as the Talbot in 1864 and kept the name until its closure early in the 20th century.

Chastleton. A fine Jacobean house built and occupied by a wealthy wool merchant from Witney and his family. The house has a grand oak staircase, many elaborate rooms, and must have employed many servants below-stairs as was the custom in bygone days.

Deddington. In the early part of the 20th century, travellers leaving Deddington and heading south would have passed two well-known landmarks: Turnpike Cottage at the bottom of the hill, and the Fox and Crown public house at the top. The photograph shows Turnpike Cottage being demolished in about 1928. A Mr R. Kearsey had bought it for £50. He used the materials to build a bungalow along the Hempton Road.

Council houses. The building of council houses was widespread just after World War One. These were built at Wroxton around 1920 by Henry Boot of Sheffield. Many local tradesman were employed on the site, including the Price brothers from Drayton; Jack Palmer and son, bricklayers; Harry Gilkes, scaffolder; and Harry and Ernest Hancox, stonemasons. It is interesting to note the fashion: everyone is wearing either a cap or a trilby.

Gambon's Mill. This mill, which was recorded in the *Domesday Book* of 1086, is on the eastern edge of the parish of North Aston. The mill was held by the Gambon family for most of the 13th century, and was called Gambon's Mill until late in the 18th century. The double mill seems to have been in use from the late 16th century until the early 18th century. The Rose family were the millers from the middle of the 17th century until 1938. By 1955 the mill had been converted for private use, although restored machinery remained in the building until 1980.

Glympton. A pretty summer scene showing Glympton Vicarage and the River Glyme, around 1930. The Vicarage belonged to the Oxford Diocese until 1961, before being sold to a private buyer, Dr Graham Swift, who lived there until 1995. The house now belongs to the Glympton Park Estate.

Milton. Joseph George Bennett, born in 1870, was the seventh child of a master shoemaker. He and his wife, Elizabeth Mary, had eight children, all born and brought up in this thatched cottage with its distinctive 14th-century doorway. One of the children was Mr Arthur Bennett, who would often recall his early childhood and how they managed with just three bedrooms.

Almshouses are mediaeval in origin. Built to provide accommodation for the aged or needy, they were founded by religious guilds or local benefactors, and were therefore distinct from publicly financed poorhouses or workhouses.

Burford almshouses. The almshouses in Burford were built between 1456 and 1476, and claim Richard Earl of Warwick as their founder. However, the true founder is said to have been Henry Bishop, who gave money to build almshouses for the poor of the town. Bishop only received permission from the Lord of the Manor to endow them on condition that the Earl and Countess of Warwick were named as founders. The almshouses are shown here as they were in the 1930s.

Chipping Norton almshouses. Many more alms-houses were founded in the 17th century. Those at Chipping Norton were established in 1640 by Henry Cornish for eight poor widows of the town. The inscription above the arch reads 'Remember the Poor'.

Shipton Court, Shipton-under-Wychwood. Now divided into residential flats, this beautiful Elizabethan building was built by the Lacys in 1603. It is said to be haunted by the ghost of Sir John Chandos Reade. Sir John, who owned the house in the mid-19th century, was an alcoholic who used to drink regularly with his butler. One evening the butler tried to ring for some more bottles, but Sir John, affected by the carousal, threw the bell rope over a picture. When the butler attempted to recover the rope he slipped and was impaled on a firedog. Although the question of whether the butler slipped or was pushed was raised, a verdict of accidental death was recorded. Nevertheless, Sir John never went drinking again and died a disturbed man in 1868. His ghost has often been seen since, despite the efforts of an exorcist.

Shipton-under-Wychwood. Two pretty cottages photographed around 1913. Alfred Miles, cabinet-maker and undertaker, lived in the cottage on the left for many years. His workshop was along the Ascott Road, past the gas works. Frank Coombes lived on the right. He was a well-known local man who began working for Alfred Willis' saddlery business after leaving school. Apart from service in World War One, Mr Coombes stayed with the firm all his life and finally took it over after the death of Alfred Willis in 1949.

The ancient market town of Burford, known as the 'gateway to the Cotswolds', grew rich in the Middle Ages from the Cotswold wool trade. To this day many beautiful stone houses bear witness to the town's opulent past.

The Old Rectory House, Priory Lane, Burford.
This house, together with the nearby priory, was held by the Lenthall family for about 200 years. Since 1949 the building has been used as a guest house by the community.

Burford Priory. Burford Priory is a fine old house with a history interwoven with the Harman, Tanfield, and Lenthall families. The house has undergone many changes over the centuries, and it is likely that this photograph was taken during the period of restoration work carried out by Mr Horniman, owner of the Priory from 1912 to 1932. Today, the Priory is used as a convent and is closed to the public.

Westhall Hill. Just outside Burford lies the small village of Westhall Hill, with its graceful four-gabled manor house. It is likely to have been the Bartholomews, owners of the house for most of the 17th century, who altered and enlarged the building to give it the appearance it has today.

Chapter Three

A Job of Work

Mark Quartermain. A carter who died in 1943, aged 87, after spending a lifetime with working horses. He was a true Oxfordshire man bearing an old Oxfordshire name dating back to Herbert and Robertus Quartermain, who lived in Merton in 1187.

James Robins. A ploughman and winner of many prizes at the Banbury Agricultural Association meetings. He is seen here toiling away during a long hard day in the field. A break for bread and cheese or home-cured bacon, helped down with a bottle of cold tea without milk, was taken under the hedge. The day was not finished until his workmates had been unharnessed, fed, and watered.

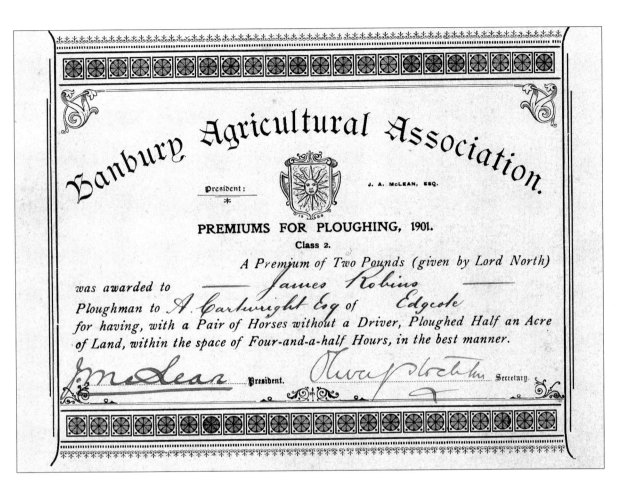

Award for ploughing. One of the many certificates awarded to James Robins.

Theodore Lamb. A true craftsman who wandered the lanes and villages of north Oxfordshire repairing clocks and watches, albeit to maintain only a poor standard of living. Although a clockmaker, he is best remembered by the locals as being a hermit who wore a sackcloth and rough home-made sandals and who lived in a shack at the side of the road. This photograph shows him paused by a heap of broken stones for road mending. His trolley was home-made and had a paraffin lantern on the front to light his way.

Village blacksmith. Charlie Coleman followed in his father's footsteps, sweating at the forge, hammering at the anvil, and shoeing horses. He is pictured here with his father Joseph, outside their blacksmith's shop in Adderbury.

Skilled farm worker, early 1920s. A farm worker mowing the meadow grass ready for making hay. After going through the hay press, the hay would be stacked, stored and then used as winter fodder. For working a 50 hour week this man would have been paid 28 shillings if he was over 21 and 25 shillings if he was under 21; 14-year-old boys would have been paid 8s 6d per week.

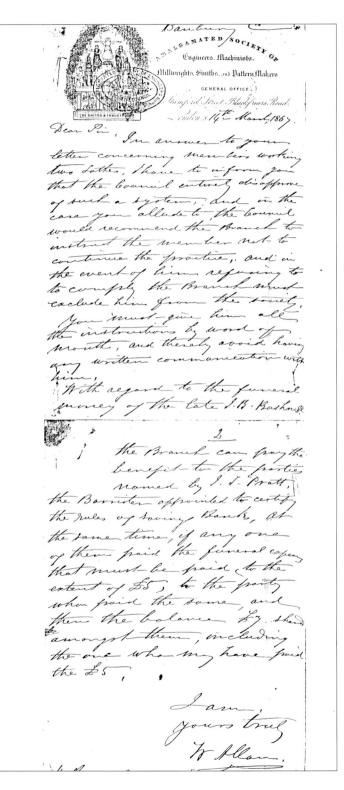

Industrial town. As Banbury changed from a market town to an industrial town the type of labour required began to change. Skilled workers in particular were now needed. In 1859 a Banbury branch of the Amalgamated Society of Engineers, Machinists, Millwrights, Smiths, and Pattern Makers was formed. The first recorded meeting was held from 8pm until 9.30pm on Saturday, 6 August 1859 at the Wheatsheaf public house, Banbury. A minute from the 20 August meeting reads, '...that a carpet bag will be supplyed [sic] to the Secretary for his use in carrying books etc. belonging to this branch from and to his home and that the branch defrays the expense.' On 11 February 1867, it was agreed that the secretary would write to the Executive Council concerning men working two lathes. The reply is dated 14 March 1867 and reads as follows, including a reference to funeral money:

Dear Sir

In answer to your letter concerning members working two lathes, I have to inform you that the Council entirely disapprove of such a system, and in the case you allude to the Council would recommend the Branch to instruct the member not to continue the practice, and in the event of him refusing to comply the Branch must exclude him from the society.

You must give him all the instructions by word of mouth, and thereby avoid having any written communication with him.

With regard to the funeral money of the late J.B. Bashnell, the Branch can pay the benefit for the parties named by J.L. Pratt, the Barrister appointed to certify the rules of savings banks, at the same time, if any one of them paid the funeral expenses that must be paid, to the extent of £5, to the party who paid the same, and then the balance £7 shared amongst them, including the one who may have paid the £5.

I am yours truly
W. Allan

Weaving factory. In this picture, taken in the early 20th century, the working women and working conditions in the huge factory room speak for themselves. The advent of power looms saw an end to weaving as a cottage industry that had been associated with the Witney area for over two centuries.

Early's of Witney, makers of fine blankets since 1669. This photograph shows Early's, the oldest blanket works in Witney, taken around 1909 from the River Windrush. Over the centuries the river has provided power for the weaving industry. What a peaceful contrast the riverside must have been from the noise and clamour of the weaving room.

Kingham. A fascinating picture of school life around 1913. Perhaps some of the people in the photograph are still alive today? What stories would they have to tell, and what did they achieve in life? Note the plants on the window ledge, the varnished roll-up pictures, and the two boys sitting with the girls, even though there is space elsewhere: this used to be a form of punishment.

T. E. Griffin, baker. In the centre of this tranquil village scene is the bread and delivery service of the day. Mr T. E. Griffin was a local baker who had his bakehouse at the side of the church at Epwell. Twice weekly he supplied the surrounding villages, including Sibford Gower where this photograph was taken. The superb stonework over the village well is the work of local stonemason, Mr Wilkes.

Man, machine and horse. Taken near Deddington around 1917, this old photograph marks a time in our history when man and machine took over from man and his horse, which had for so long sowed, reaped, and harvested the Oxfordshire countryside.

Harvest time. Taken deep in the heart of the Oxfordshire countryside at the onset of World War One, this was a familiar harvest-time scene. An old binder and early tractor are ready to reap a field of waving golden corn. Once the early sun had evaporated the morning dew, the days work could start and would not end until darkness fell. Weary workers and tired-out children would make their way home under a pale harvest moon.

On strike. In December 1913, Union members at Bliss Tweed Mill came out on a seven-month-long strike over wages and union recognition. They can be seen here marching through Chipping Norton with a banner that reads, 'We fight for liberty. Down with oppression.' Members of the strike committee were jailed at Oxford and included at least one woman. She was presented with a silver tea service by supporters on her release. Non-union workers did not want to strike, but because of the bitterness felt towards them, they had to be escorted to work by the local constabulary. It was a strike that divided the town and brought heartache to many families.

Loyal employees. A group of workers showing their intentions with a placard that reads, 'Bliss Loyal Employe's [sic].'

Deddington, around 1923. The young man second from the left is Mr Allen Course, who was born at nearby Deddington Mill. In 1932 the fire engine was housed at the town hall, which was convenient for the town well. It had previously been kept in a building on the Green.

Fire at Alfred Groves and Sons, Milton-under-Wychwood. As the photograph shows, a lot of damage was caused by the fire of 1926. Perhaps consolation would have been taken from the fact that at least the gantry's wooden structure seems to have survived intact. Notice the men to the right of the picture inspecting the debris, no doubt trying to decide what is fit for salvage. Alfred Groves and Sons Ltd., building contractors, are still in operation today, continuing a business established over 300 years ago.

Shutford. This picture of Shutford schoolgirls was taken in the early 1920s and, considering the size of the village, they must all have been present. Many probably ended up working at Wrenches thriving plush factory. One who did not was Miss Violet Turner, pictured here in the second row, fourth from the right. Instead, the young Miss Turner went into service after leaving school. The Turner family had long been associated with plush weaving in Shutford; Miss Violet Turner's father Alfred, her grandfather Amos, and her uncle William were all hand weavers at the factory.

Claydon post office. The photograph on the left shows the village post office before it moved to its new location shown on the right. The young lady on the right, outside the new post office building, is Mrs Annie Marie Prew. Born in 1889, she lived and worked at the post office during World War One. Then, as now, the Post Office was a large employer of both men and women. In 1914, around 123,000 people worked for the Post Office, accounting for over 70% of all Civil Service employment. Claydon village post office later returned to the original building. Today the sub-post office is housed in a modern building along the road to Boddington.

Banbury cattle market. This superb postcard was posted in May 1904. Cattle can be seen in front of the town hall, and by the footpath railings. Nearby, carrier's carts await the return home. Notice the crowd gathered outside the town hall for the auction. No doubt throughout the day many deals would be struck as well as news and gossip exchanged; this was an important community gathering. Cattle were sold in the streets of Banbury for the last time in 1931. The cattle market then moved from Cow Fair to purpose-built premises in Grimsbury.

The Tolsey in Burford High Street, around 1905. During the Middle Ages Burford was run by a Guild of Merchants who were entitled to hold a market and collect tolls from anyone wishing to trade in the town. It was the Guild of Merchants who built the Tolsey, or toll-house, sometime before 1561, as a place to hold meetings and receive tolls. In 1617 Sir Lawrence Tanfield bought the Lordship of the Manor and successfully took the Guild to court for usurping the rights of the Lord of the Manor. As a consequence, Tanfield became so unpopular that following his death in 1625, his effigy was burnt in the High Street every Midsummer's Day for 200 years.

Slatters and Olivers. In the mid 1920s, Long Hanborough boasted two garages: Slatters and Olivers. The latter was started in 1919 by Harry Oliver, with just one Model-T Ford. He is pictured here outside his garage with various vehicles for sale and hire. For many years the company also used the building opposite, previously the parish hall, as a workshop. The garage moved to its present position on the south side of Main Road in the mid 1960s. Today, John Oliver, son of Harry, continues the family business.

Chipping Norton Red Cross Hospital. Taken during World War One, when cameras were far from commonplace, this lasting record of social history was the work of the Chipping Norton photographer Mr Frank Packer. Many old Oxfordshire scenes would be lost forever, or exist only in fading memories, if it had not been for the work of local photographers such as Percy Simms, Frank Packer, and later his son Basil Packer. The present-day local historian owes much to the work of such men.

Chapter Four
Transport

Steam railways. Very few aspects of life were left untouched by the coming of the railways and steam locomotion. Heavy goods could now be carried long distances at speed, and people could cross the country in hours instead of days. In the 1920s, even cross country lines like this one at Chipping Norton were busy places, with supplies being brought in for the town and nearly all the visitors, post and cattle travelling by rail. Horse-drawn drays were used to haul deliveries up New Street to the town centre. The line from Chipping Norton to Kings Sutton closed to passengers in June 1951; the Great Western line from Kingham to Chipping Norton closed to all traffic in December 1962.

Great Western, London and North Western Railway station. Banbury, about 1854. During World War One the station, although short of staff, handled many troop trains. In February 1915, upwards of 12,000 of the London NW Company's staff had responded to the nation's call, as well as some 10,000 of the Great Western staff.

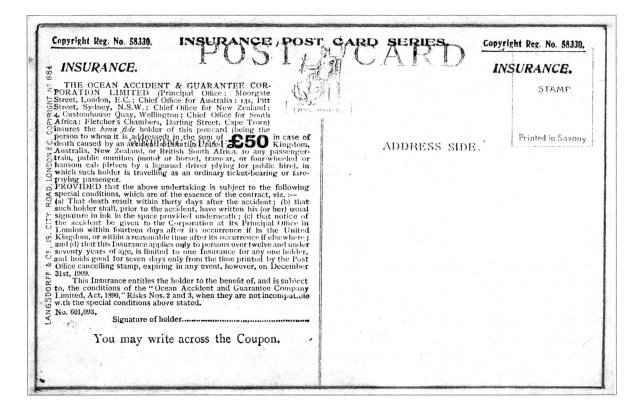

Insurance policy. The reverse side of a postcard of Oxfordshire that acted as an insurance policy should the purchaser die as a result of an accident caused by a passenger train, public omnibus (motor or horse), tramcar, or other form of public transport. The insurance was valid on purchase of the postcard, and covered seven days from the date of the Post Office cancelling stamp. This particular postcard was valid for the year 1909.

Carrier's carts. During Victorian and Edwardian times, carrier's carts provided a vital means of transportation and communication between villages and towns. North Oxfordshire was no exception, with the people of Banburyshire making regular use of carrier's carts to travel to Banbury to exchange goods and news. One of the many carriers was William Gregory Bason, pictured here in 1908 outside St Mary's church in Banbury. William Bason's regular service connected Milton, Adderbury, and Banbury.

Pony and Trap. What better way to illustrate the pace of life than this postcard, posted in 1912. It was a long, hot summer that year, as indicated by the dry mud bank and confirmed by the resident of No. 14, Taynton who wrote, 'I expect you know what view this is, its the bridge round the old way. We are having it very hot now, makes work go hard. Father said he's been over that bridge many a time.'

Miss Susie Tustain. Newspapers of the day carried adverts depicting young ladies in pretty clothes riding bicycles, encouraging women to take up cycling as a hobby. But in real rural areas the bicycle was a way of life, not a hobby, whether used to post a letter, visit the vicar, or fetch the doctor. When Miss Susie Tustain was more than three score years and ten she would often reflect, 'What would I have done without the bike?'

Meeting of the four shires. This monument marks the meeting of the four shires: Oxfordshire, Warwickshire, Worcestershire, and Gloucestershire. The stone can still be seen today, situated about six miles north-west of Chipping Norton on the A44. However, as a result of county boundary changes, it no longer marks the meeting of the four shires.

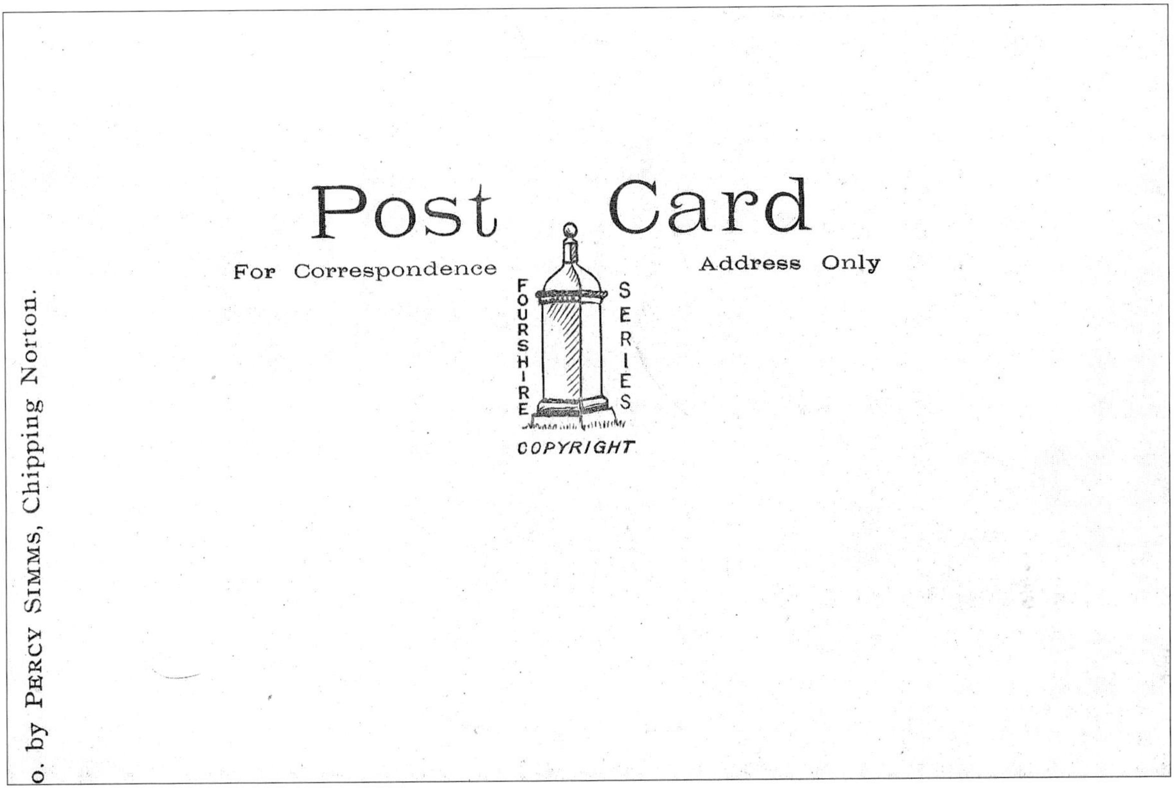

Post . Card

For Correspondence

Address Only

F O U R S H I R E

S E R I E S

COPYRIGHT

o. by PERCY SIMMS, Chipping Norton.

Four shires postcards. A series of postcards depicting scenes from the four shires was produced by Percy Simms between the late 1920s and the early 1930s. Each one had the four shires logo printed on the back.

A bright cold morning. This is 1916, the third winter into World War One, and the local men have been busy clearing nature's work. Snow was a much longed for event among the children, as much then as it is today, especially if it meant a morning off school because of blocked roads. However, the little chap on the left seems to have had enough and is probably thinking of his warm home and mum's cooking.

Chipping Norton crossroads. This photograph was taken on a clear, tranquil summer's day sometime before 1918. The faithful horse had been the main form of local transport for many centuries, but soon the first motor vehicles would be regularly disturbing these graceful, tree-lined tracks and roads. From this point, traders could travel north-east to Banbury cattle market, later to become the largest in Europe, or south-east to Oxford, passing through Enstone and Woodstock along

Bletchingdon crossroads. This postcard shows the main road to Hampton Poyle and Oxford. The Red Lion public house to the left of the picture must have been a welcome retreat for the commercial traveller. It would have provided a break from the hot dusty road, and a chance to exchange news and gossip over some much deserved liquid refreshment. The Halls public house was run by the Barratt sisters until the early 1950s. Today the building is a private house.

Witney High Street. Close inspection of this charming postcard reveals some of the numerous ways in which people and goods were carried in the first decade of the 20th century. The solidly built horse-drawn dray, ironically pictured here outside a temperance hotel, belonged to Hitchman's brewery, a long-established Chipping Norton company. With branches in Worcester, Stratford-upon-Avon, Warwick, Blockley, Evesham, and Oxford, Hitchman's drays must have been a common sight gently winding their way along the county's roads. Hitchman's brewery closed in 1932, having been a major employer in Chipping Norton since 1796.

Charlbury toll house. During the 17th century the increase in popularity of coach transport began to seriously affect the county's road network. Many roads were little more than rough tracks and could not withstand the increased wear and tear. In an attempt to organise road repair, turnpike trusts were set up. The trusts financed road repair by raising money from tolls. The first turnpike trust in Oxfordshire was set up in 1718, and covered the London road from Oxford to Stokenchurch. The road from Charlbury to Witney was turnpiked in 1800. The growth of the railways in the 19th century caused a decline in coach travel, and by around 1878 most turnpike trusts had run out of funds and were disbanded. Tollhouses were usually round or octagonal so that the keeper had windows facing up and down the road as well as towards the gate.

Banbury Cross and St Mary's church. This photograph is likely to have been taken in the early to mid 1920s. The relatively new-looking statues of Queen Victoria, Edward VII, and George V were installed in 1914 to mark the coronation of George V in 1911. In 1888 the cross was redecorated, new gaslights were installed, and iron railings erected. These were removed in 1927. The general layout of this part of Banbury has not changed significantly since the photograph was taken. Today however, it would be difficult to capture such a quiet scene, with its uncrowded roads and solitary Midland Red bus.

Burford High Street. This photograph was clearly taken at an age when the motor vehicle had started to dominate the town's main streets. Notice the six motor cars, a motorcycle, a motorcycle with sidecar, and a public motorbus as well as various items of street furniture.

Chipping Norton High Street, around 1908. In this rare photographic postcard it looks as if the whole town has stopped their daily business to come and look at an electric light standard that has been knocked over by a motor car. For the moment however, the townsfolk's interest seems to lie more in the opportunity to be in a photograph than with the fallen light.

Charabanc. Originating in France and literally meaning 'wagon with benches', charabancs became a popular form of motor transport following World War One. This photograph was taken in Chipping Norton during a parish church Bible class outing to Windsor. What an experience it must have been for the women on board. They certainly seem in high spirits on what appears to be a glorious summer's day. Notice the large hood at the back of the vehicle however, which acted as a safeguard lest the weather should turn.

Motorcycle and side-car. This photograph, taken around 1926, shows Rose Trinder and her daughter Joan next to a BSA (Birmingham Small Arms) Big Twin motorcycle and sidecar combination. Such vehicles were used extensively throughout the 1920s, when the cost of purchasing even a small private motor car was prohibitive to the vast majority of working people. In 1906, Joan Trinder's grandfather, William Edward Trinder, opened a shop in Broad Street, Banbury, selling motorcycles and bicycles. Although no longer connected with the family, Trinders toy-shop still trades in Broad Street today.

Chapter Five
Recreation and Pastimes

South Newington, Barford, and Wigginton Flower Show, 1929. Although these events were called flower shows, they covered most garden produce. Typical entries would be:

Potatoes (white kidney)	Prize 1lb of tea.
Apples (culinary)	Prize 2s 6d.
Window plants	First prize 3s, second prize 2s.
Field grasses as a bouquet	Prize 3s.
Cut white flowers	First prize 3s, second prize 2s.
Boiled potatoes	First prize cotton dress, second prize 2s.
Beetroot	Prize 2s 6d.

The best collection of vegetables, 8 varieties, one variety to be 6 different sorts of potatoes of 9 tubers each.

First prize 12s 6d, second prize 7s 6d.

School holidays. Time to explore the fields and spinneys, pick cowslips in the meadow, and catch sticklebacks in a jam jar at the brook. This photograph, taken in the early 1930s, shows the boys with poke caps and girls with hats, one of them hoping she has caught something from the stream.

Camping trip. Girl Guides from Bloxham out on the open road and looking fortunate enough to be getting a helping hand. It looks like a warm evening as the sun is casting long shadows; maybe they are making their way to Broughton Castle to camp. Many Girl Guide and Boy Scout camps took place in the castle fields, encouraged by Lord and Lady Saye and Sele.

The Princess Mary, photographed around the time of World War One. Usually called a traction engine, this mighty showmans road locomotive has its chimney stacked and canvas tied ready to go to the next town fair. The owner, a regular visitor to Oxfordshire fairs, is W. Nichols, amusement contractor, 115 Pevensey Road, Forest Gate.

Harvest festival. Even at a time when religion played a greater part in most people's lives, it would have been difficult to find a more splendid harvest festival display and decorated citadel than this one by the Salvation Army in 1930.

Leafield fête. This photograph, taken in the 1920s, shows what a popular event these annual fêtes were. Apart from a day out for the children, it could have been a fashion parade. A lot of planning and organising went into these events for weeks before the day.

Milton, around 1935. Most children had to make their own amusement during the summer holidays and one of the most popular was dressing up. A favourite with the girls was pretending to get married and, as can be seen, a great deal of care was taken to make it realistic, the parents having been pestered for anything from grannies old things to the lace curtains.

Witney feast fair. The following was written to Mr E.R. Hawkes, 66 Cardigan Street, St Barnabas, Oxford on 15 September 1909. 'Dear Ern, Witney feast fair very dull this year pouring wet Monday enjoyed ourselves in the haunted house Flo Taylor nearly had a fit when we got out just kept her from going right off. Best love from Flo.'

Kingham. The Women's Institute was a way of life, with branches in villages and towns all over the country. They maintained traditional values and kept their standards high. They had market stalls, organised whist drives, and had talks by invited speakers. In many places they were the hub of the social and craft side of life.

Collecting postcards. Until the outbreak of World War One, collecting postcards was a favourite pastime among the working classes as it was inexpensive and a means of keeping in touch. Some of the best collections were created by domestic servants.

POST CARD

THIS SPACE MAY BE USED
FOR COMMUNICATION
IN THE BRITISH ISLES ONLY.
(Post Office Regulation.)

THE ADDRESS ONLY TO BE
WRITTEN HERE.

Printed in Saxony

I Thought this
would do. for
your. collection
I got home.
safe. found all
well hope you
did. yours M.

Miss Allen.
Wells Lodge.
Holkham Park.
Nr Wells
Norfolk

Postcard from a friend. The reverse side of this card shows Wroxton Abbey. A domestic servant from the Abbey sent it to her friend, also in service, at Holkham Park in 1906.

Leap-frog. A bright sunny day for a game of leap-frog, but only for the boys. Girls were not allowed and had to play at skipping or hopscotch, that is, of course, unless they were needed to make the numbers up or one was willing to always be jumped over. Then it was agreed, 'We'll let them play then', after all mother had said that nobody was to be left out.

Boy Scouts. Nearly every schoolboy at sometime or another wanted to belong to the local Boy Scout group. It was one of the few organisations that met regularly, provided training, taught skills, and fostered a spirit of comradeship. The photograph shows either first aid training or, more probably as this is the 1915 Scout rally at Chadlington, a team entered into a competition.

Steeple Barton, 1929. Memories and records tell us that folk dancing must have been popular in the county for many generations, and while there has not always been continuity, the art does not seem to have been lost. The maiden in the centre of this group of folk dancers now lives at Horspath and remembers the occasion well.

May Day. Festivities, such as crowning the May Queen and dancing around the maypole, have been with us for generations. There are many variations of the songs and flower arrangements, but what a splendid picture of May Day at Heythrop in 1912.

May Day at Over Norton, 1937. Notice the expressions on the children's faces as they pose for a photograph around the maypole. Seasoned gardeners will tell you that 12 May is the old May Day and the day to plant the kidney-bean seed.

Donkey derby. Between the wars working-class people could not afford seaside holidays, so they had to make the most of local entertainment. Events boasting donkey rides were sure of drawing large crowds. A variation on the donkey ride was the donkey derby, where donkeys were raced to win. Travelling showmen would sometimes supply the donkeys and graze them on the outskirts of the village, usually on the grassy roadside verges. This donkey derby was held in Deddington in 1925.

Souldern club, 1909. Friendly societies were a form of mutual aid for country people, and the club walks held each year were important events in village life. Members would be decorated with flowers and carry banners and poles. Membership came from all walks of life and spanned at least three generations.

The small village of Church Enstone. This photograph of church club day was taken in the summer of 1908. The local band and some of the club members are making their way up the Bicester Road towards the church of St Kenelm. Club days were important events in village life. They brought together members of the community as well as providing an opportunity for clubs to advertise and recruit new members. Considering the size of the village, the event was clearly well supported. Many generations must have worshipped at the church of St Kenelm since the original church building was erected over 1,000 years ago. The church is unusual in that it has a ninth-century King of Mercia as its patron saint.

The Friendly Society. This Friendly Society gathering of 1912 in the small village of Leafield must have been quite an event. Around 100 ladies are present, so few of the women of the village would have been left out. With the Suffragette Movement making headlines and World War One only two years away, the lives of these women were to change dramatically in the decade that followed.

Chipping Norton. This photographic postcard, taken in 1929, shows local people from Chipping Norton and surrounding villages enjoying the icy conditions caused by the coldest February for more than 30 years. Present-day visitors to the town will be unsuccessful should they try to find Chipping Norton Lake. This is not surprising, since the lake used to be created deliberately for winter recreation by flooding the common land to the west of the town, known as Pool Meadow. Such flooding has not taken place for many years, and today a tree-lined stream and small stone bridge locate the original site.

North Newington youth hostel. During the 1920s and 1930s the advent of affordable private motor cars, and the increase in public transport, changed the way in which people spent their leisure time. Holiday opportunities increased and countless public and private enterprises were created to cater for demand. The Youth Hostels Association for England and Wales was founded in 1930 to foster a love of the countryside by providing hostels and other simple accommodation. The farmhouse hostel at North Newington opened in the spring of 1933, with Mr and Mrs Hutchings as wardens. Accommodation was originally for 10 males and 10 females, with sleeping bags available for hire. The hostel closed in the summer of 1948.

Chipping Norton. The National Children's Home and Orphanage was a voluntary organisation established in 1873 to care for destitute children. A branch of the NCH & O opened in New Street in 1904. The annual fête provided a good source of income for the home, as well as a chance for the children to escape their normally austere and disciplined life. In this scene from the fête of 1917 we see a collection of beautifully made Post Office items for sale, including postcards. Collectors of such items may wish to consider how much that same display would sell for at auction today.

The decorated pram competition. Another scene from the National Children's Home and Orphanage fête of 1917. Notice the band playing in the background.

Family holiday. Car ownership opened up new possibilities for family holidays. Mrs Joan Blann (née Trinder), pictured here with her mother and Aunt, clearly recalls her childhood camping holidays in the early 1930s. The family would drive from Banbury to the Hampshire coast in their Austin 7 and their Morris Minor with a large trailer in tow.

Burford High Street. This sepia photograph was taken outside the Tolsey on meet day. The meet was a regular event, and the huntsman's horn was often heard between November and March. Children were allowed to follow the hunt on foot or by bicycle, as long as they kept quiet and did not get in the way.

Ascott-under-Wychwood football club. This photograph was taken during an era when many people worked in shops, banks, offices, and factories on Saturday mornings. Like today, most towns and villages had a football and cricket team, and the afternoon sporting events brought a welcome end to the working week. Here we see Ascott-under-Wychwood Football Club, winners of the Wychwood League 1927-28. The goalkeeper was Mr H. Clark, and Mr G. Hambidge holds the cup.

Chapter Six
The Effects of War

Claydon. This superb photograph was taken outside Claydon post office in 1914. The Army recruitment poster urges 'Any smart lad' to join the Oxfordshire Light Infantry. Other posters, produced by the Parliamentary Recruiting Committee, appealed to the women of Britain to encourage their men to enlist. Many Oxfordshire men took the 'King's Shilling' in August 1914, helping to bring Britain's total enlistment to an astounding 250,000 within the first five weeks of the war.

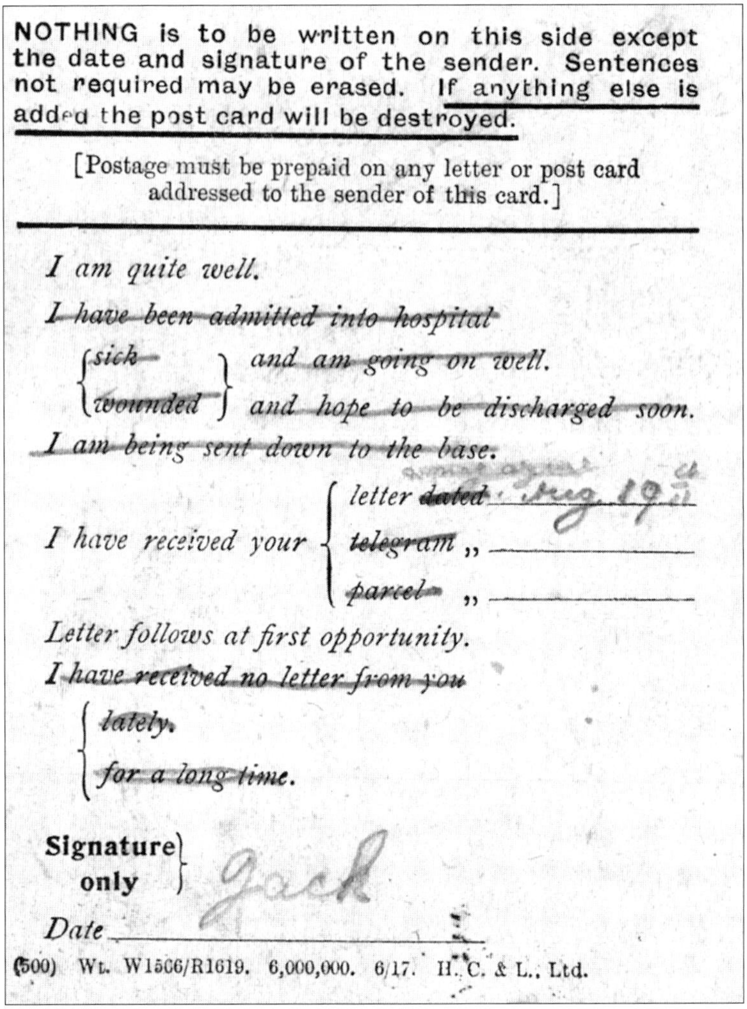

NOTHING is to be written on this side except the date and signature of the sender. Sentences not required may be erased. If anything else is added the post card will be destroyed.

[Postage must be prepaid on any letter or post card addressed to the sender of this card.]

I am quite well.

~~*I have been admitted into hospital*~~

~~{ *sick* }~~ ~~*and am going on well.*~~
~~{ *wounded* }~~ ~~*and hope to be discharged soon.*~~

~~*I am being sent down to the base.*~~

I have received your { *letter* ~~*dated*~~ *Aug. 19*
telegram ,, _____
~~*parcel*~~ *,,* _____ }

Letter follows at first opportunity.

~~*I have received no letter from you*~~

~~{ *lately.*~~

~~{ *for a long time.*~~

Signature only } *Jack*

Date _____

(500) Wt. W1566/R1619. 6,000,000. 6/17. H. C. & L., Ltd.

Postcard from the front. An Oxfordshire lad fighting in the trenches during World War One sent this postcard to his sister in Banbury. It was posted from a field post office in France on 20 August 1917. Should the card have fallen into the wrong hands, it would have been of little use since no surname, rank, regiment, or area of battle is shown. It is simply from a soldier somewhere in France.

Oxfordshire soldiers. Old family photograph albums and treasured letters bear witness to the fact that many Oxfordshire men fought in Flanders and the Somme during World War One. These photographic postcards shown were sold in aid of the Blinded Soldiers' Children Fund.

Oxfordshire regiments. Following the declaration of war against Germany on 4 August 1914, the Queen's Own Oxfordshire Hussars, the Oxfordshire and Buckinghamshire Light Infantry, the National Reserve, and Army and Navy Reservists were immediately mobilised. Many young Oxfordshire men were prepared to fight. Born in Milton in 1885, Joseph Henry Bason served with the 11th Hussars as a despatch rider.

Bill Mobley. Born in Banbury in 1900, Thomas William (Bill) Mobley was one of the 2,161 Banburians who served in the forces during World War One. He served with the Army Service Corps in France, and was later posted to Germany with the Rhine Signals Battalion as part of the Allied occupation of the Rhineland. The treaty of Versailles had placed the Rhineland under Allied control and designated it a demilitarised zone, out of bounds to German forces for a maximum term of 15 years. The last Allied detachments left in 1930.

Harry Mobley. Born in Banbury in 1898, George Henry (Harry) Mobley, brother of Bill, served with the Royal Engineers in France as a driver. This photograph was taken to commemorate his receiving a medal for the best-turned out soldier and horse. Harry Mobley was one of the 325 men from Banbury who fell during the war. He is commemorated on a Commonwealth War Graves Commission memorial in the town of Soissons, France. The memorial is mainly dedicated to the British officers and men who were killed during the summer of 1918, when the town fell to Germany. It records nearly 4,000 World War One casualties whose graves are not known.

Red Cross collection. Posted in Chipping Norton in June 1915, this postcard shows Red Cross nurses collecting funds during World War One. Funds collected were used by the International Committee of the Red Cross to provide relief to prisoners of war, and many Red Cross parcels were sent to such prisoners. The two boys at the front look as if they are ready to enlist. Maybe their country called upon them later on in life when once again the world was at war.

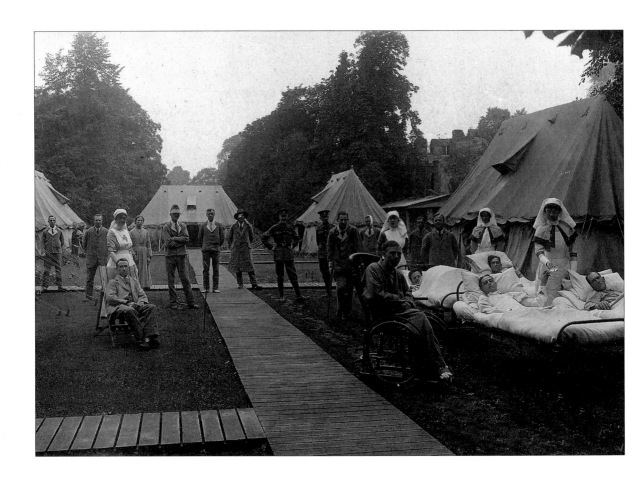

Garden hospital. During World War One, various Oxford University buildings were used as part of the Third Southern General Hospital. On 17 August 1914, a meeting of Warden and Fellows of New College Oxford agreed to allow the erection of hospital tents in the college garden for the duration of the war. This postcard shows a few of the many men who were nursed to recovery by hospital staff. Although the hospital itself closed in December 1919, for some of the shell-shocked victims it would be many years before they could come to terms with their experiences in the trenches of the Western Front.

Protection Certificate and Certificate of Identity. This certificate was issued to H.J. Robins on his discharge from the Army in 1919. The postmaster would stamp the bottom of the certificate after receiving a payment of two pounds a week for four weeks. The Army pay then stopped and a job had to be found.

Witney peace celebrations. On Saturday 19 July 1919, peace celebrations were held all over the country. Witney was no exception, and the townspeople worked hard to make the day a memorable occasion. There was a children's procession in the afternoon, and a dinner held for about 250 discharged and demobilised sailors and soldiers in the Corn Exchange in the evening. The photograph, taken prior to the banquet, shows the hall prettily decorated with flags of all nationalities, and the tables adorned with flowers. Over the platform, worked in flowers, are the words, 'Welcome home to our brave boys'. The dinner comprised soup, roast beef and mutton, cherry pies, gooseberry pies, jam tarts, jellies, and blancmanges.

Memorial service, Milton-under-Wychwood. A typical English church with its large stone columns and arches, stained-glass windows, and long wooden pews. Here, and elsewhere, the men who fought for King and Country were remembered. Memorial services took place in churches all over the county, and it is hard today to find a town, village, or hamlet without a war memorial. Forty-two men fell during World War One from the parishes of Milton-under-Wychwood, Bruern and Lyneham.

Fulbrook war memorial. A memorial to the eight men from the village who gave their lives during World War One. The inscription on the front face reads, 'These are the men from Fulbrook who died that we might live. 1914-1918. Faithful unto death.' The fallen are also remembered in a roll of honour displayed in the nearby Norman church of St James the Great.

Chipping Norton War Memorial Hospital. After the end of World War One, it was agreed that a hospital should be built as a war memorial. The hospital could be used by the town and surrounding villages and would do away with the need to travel to Banbury or Oxford for treatment. Funds were raised from donations, subscriptions, collection boxes, and the yearly hospital carnival. The War Memorial Hospital opened in 1920. Of course, patients had to pay for treatment, as this was long before the days of the National Health Service. The photograph shows Lady Margaret Watney opening the maternity ward in 1929.

Select Bibliography

General

Cecil, R. *Life in Edwardian England*. Batsford, London (1969).

May, T. *Agriculture and Rural Society in Britain 1846-1914*. Arnold, London (1973).

Mingay, G.E. *Rural Life in Victorian England*. Heinemann, London (1977).

Royle, E. *Modern Britain – A Social History 1750-1985*. Arnold, London (1987).

Terraine, J. *Impacts of War 1914-1918*. Hutchinson, London (1970).

Oxfordshire

Jessup, M. *A History of Oxfordshire*. Phillimore, Chichester (1975).

Ward Lock Red Guide *The Cotswolds*. Ward Lock (1970).

Williams, E. C. *Companion into Oxfordshire*. Methuen, London (1935).

Penguin Guides *Berks & Oxon*. Penguin Books, London (1950).

The Victoria History of the County of Oxford. Oxford University Press, Oxford.

Bloxham, C. *Portrait of Oxfordshire*. Robert Hale, London (1982).

Oxfordshire Town & Village Index

KINFOLK

info@kinfolk.com
www.kinfolk.com

Published by Ouur Media
Amagertorv 14, Level 1
1160 Copenhagen, Denmark

5210 N Williams Avenue
Portland, Oregon 97217 USA
Telephone: 503-946-8400

Printed in Canada

Publication Design by Charlotte Heal
Cover Photograph by Pelle Crépin

MADE & CRAFTED™
LEVI'S®

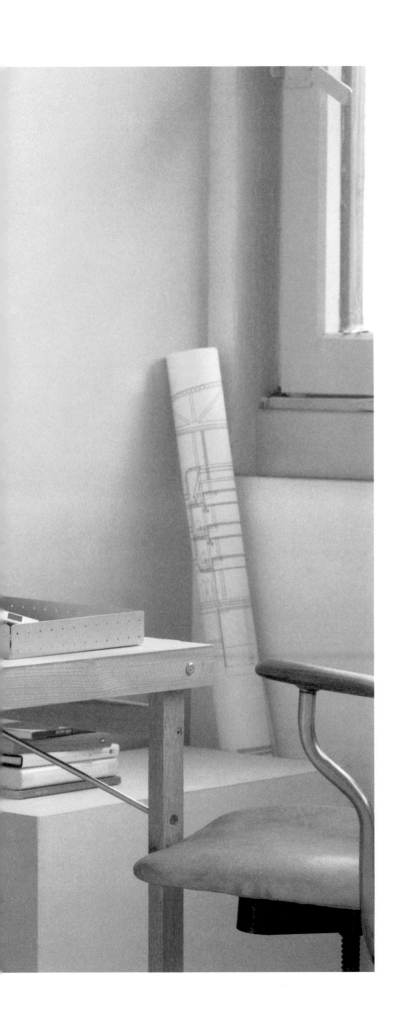

LG MUSIC flow

An Essential Part of My Everyday

Life's Good

SUNSPEL.COM

SUNSPEL

ENGLAND 1860

LEANDRA MEDINE
founder of Man Repeller

ISSUE Nº
FOSSIL
1954

CALLING ALL CURIOUS
WWW.FOSSIL.COM

NEIL BEDFORD
Photographer
London, United Kingdom

NICOLE FRANZEN
Photographer
Brooklyn, New York

ADRIENNE MATEI
Writer
Vancouver, Canada

AUSTIN BRYANT
Writer
Boston, Massachusetts

AVI FRIEDMAN
Writer
Montréal, Canada

SARAH OWEN
Writer
Brooklyn, New York

DIANA BUDDS
Writer
Brooklyn, New York

CHRISTIAN FRIIS
Photographer
Copenhagen, Denmark

CAMILLA POLE
Stylist
London, United Kingdom

SARAH BUNTER
Casting Director
London, United Kingdom

DAN GLASSER
Photographer
London, United Kingdom

MANDY REP
Art Director
Copenhagen, Denmark

KATRIN COETZER
Illustrator
Cape Town, South Africa

JOANNA HAN
Writer
Brooklyn, New York

SOUKÉNA ROUSSI
Stylist
Brooklyn, New York

PELLE CRÉPIN
Photographer
London, United Kingdom

RUTH HIGGINBOTHAM
Stylist
London, United Kingdom

SIDSEL RUDOLPH
Stylist
Copenhagen, Denmark

DANIELLE DEMETRIOU
Writer
Tokyo, Japan

THOMAS HOWARD
Producer
London, United Kingdom

ANDERS SCHØNNEMANN
Photographer
Copenhagen, Denmark

PHIL DUNLOP
Photographer
London, United Kingdom

SARA INGEMANN
Stylist
Copenhagen, Denmark

DANIEL SCHRIVER
Photographer
Copenhagen, Denmark

MARGARET EVERTON
Writer
Portland, Oregon

MIKKEL KARSTAD
Recipe Writer
Copenhagen, Denmark

MATTHEW SPROUT
Photographer
New York, New York

JUSTIN FANTL
Photographer
Los Angeles, California

JORDAN KUSHINS
Writer
San Francisco, California

SADIE STEIN
Writer
New York, New York

MAIA FLORE
Photographer
Paris, France

NOEL MANALILI
Photographer
Paris, France

ZOLTAN TOMBOR
Photographer
Brooklyn, New York

unimproved

THE NAVY CHAIR
Handmade in America from recycled aluminum
since 1944. Tested to last 150 years.
emeco.net

WELCOME

————

Design is a type of communication. It's about the way an object or idea speaks to its audience. But good design not only gets its message across—it also engages us in a conversation.

For the Design Issue of *Kinfolk*, we explore the relationship between community and design. How can design strengthen bonds with our families, friends and neighbors? And how can good design improve our quality of life? After all, design doesn't just refer to the objects we surround ourselves with: Other areas of our lives can be improved with a little dose of creative malleability.

We asked some industry experts to explain the benefits of participatory design, neighborhood planning, the psychology of desirability and the power of public libraries. They all stressed that the emotional side of creativity is just as important as the physical outcomes it produces, so we've also included essays on innovation's more esoteric aspects, such as the importance of empathy, the best ways to brainstorm and how thinking like a designer can make us happier.

We delved into some of design's core elements: The results include a photo essay on how the geometric patterns in sports fields keep us in shape, an article researching symmetry in nature, a monochromatic menu made entirely using black and white ingredients and a portrait series surveying the opposite end of the spectrum—the evocative power of color.

This issue's excerpt was taken from Avi Friedman's inquisitive book *A View From the Porch*. It investigates the chicken-and-egg question of modern interior design: Does the design of our homes influence how we live in them, or are shifting social trends changing the way we design our homes? To discuss this mind-bender further, we asked Ilse Crawford and Hugo Macdonald of StudioIlse to give their two cents' worth.

For our first-ever feature profile, we spent a few days with artist Michele Oka Doner, a sculptor and author who has spent 70 years fortifying her relationship with nature—even while living in the middle of New York. We also grouped together quintessentially British fashion designer Margaret Howell, Brooklyn-based interactive installation experts Snarkitecture, French architects Studio KO, Taiwan-born graphic designer Natasha Jen and the Danish/Swedish duo behind design firm All the Way to Paris for a profile series about how community plays a central role in everything that they do.

The voices in the following pages have taught us that there's no set of rules that govern what constitutes "good design." Form doesn't have to follow function, function doesn't have to follow form—in fact, there shouldn't be any following at all, only leading. And this is the best way that design can truly serve the communities it is imagined for.

————

NATHAN WILLIAMS AND GEORGIA FRANCES KING

www.lapaz.pt

LA PAZ

Starters

The Design Issue

Starters

WORDS
RACHEL EVA LIM

Happiness by Design

———

Sometimes we should all think like designers: The strategies employed to create a perfectly proportioned bookshelf can also be used to enhance our personal well-being.

Happiness is often viewed as an ethereal and esoteric concept— a feeling that's more governed by destiny and circumstance than the product of a well-developed scheme. But living a fulfilled life is mostly within our control, and it's highly receptive to strategies inspired by creative disciplines. By borrowing from the way designers solve problems—sometimes referred to as *design thinking*—we can generate innovative solutions for achieving greater happiness.

The conversation regarding the relationship between design and happiness has gained traction in recent years. Whether it's a witty billboard that makes us chuckle on our commute to work or a chaise lounge perfectly contoured to our spine, the objects and experiences that get the little details right can boost our appreciation of both the world around us and ourselves.

Designers such as Stefan Sagmeister situate happiness as a defining aspect of their work. The firm that he co-founded, Sagmeister & Walsh, advocates bringing back emotion, human-centeredness and delight into a design culture that has trended toward the belief that functionality trumps form. "It was a subject that most roads I was exploring seemed to be leading to," says Sagmeister, whose recent projects include *The Happy Show* and *The Happy Film*. "I thought it would be interesting to look at it through the lens of my own profession."

Surrounding ourselves with carefully crafted contraptions can add a significant amount of pleasure to our lives, but we can also take a cue from designers themselves to learn how to be the architects of our own happiness. Design thinking isn't confined to creative studios, and many of its fundamental methods are applicable in other areas of life. Much as an architect examines his or her environment and attempts to solve problems through constructions, we can take stock of our personal situations and employ a similar set of design-thinking strategies to increase our happiness.

Academics engaged in happiness research agree that much of our emotional well-being lies within our direct control. A study conducted by psychologist Sonja Lyubomirsky concluded that happiness is 50 percent genetic, 40 percent intentional and 10 percent circumstantial: This means a happier state of mind is perfectly attainable—so long as we're willing to put in the work.

One of the key methods some designers adopt to overcome creative blocks is called *divergent thinking*. This thought process facilitates innovation and creativity by exploring options rather than adhering to a rigid compendium of rules. Like design, happiness isn't one-size-fits-all, and we need to consider our own needs rather than resorting to people-pleasing solutions. Similarly, products designed for the masses without considering individuals— everything from right-handed fountain pens to "flesh-colored" Band-Aids—often leave a significant percentage of the population wanting. When it comes to our individual happiness, we need to keep our minds open instead of blindly following the pack—what *actually* brings us joy rarely aligns with what *should* make us happy.

Both happiness and design also require constant upkeep. Designers toil tirelessly to birth the perfect invention, but they have to continually refine their products to respond to shifting social conditions. We can't fall victim to complacency; just as trends come and go, our needs and wants also evolve. We need to consistently check ourselves to see if the path we're on is still the right one—and if it's not, then we should take charge and change tack.

Although modifying our tried and trusted routines can seem intimidating, experimenting with new ways of thinking can be the spark we need to recalibrate our emotions. By stepping out of our comfort zones and testing design-thinking strategies, we're able to implement a variety of creative techniques that can bring a heightened sense of happiness, purpose and joy into our lives.

HAPPINESS BY DESIGN: Can by Casalinga; bowl and glass bottle by Menu; cup by HAY; round bowl by Studio Arhoj; glass by Notre Dame.

WORDS
MARY STUTZMAN

Lagom

*Not too much, not too little—
this Scandinavian term
describes being perfectly happy
to be stuck in the middle.*

LANGUAGE: Swedish

PRONUNCIATION: "La-gome" (rhymes with home)

ETYMOLOGY: From the phrase *laget om*, meaning "around the team"

MEANING: A cross between Goldilocks and the golden mean, *lagom* combines the idea of "just right" with an awareness of the greater good. It's the internal ruler that measures moderation so that there'll always be enough for others. According to folklore, lagom stems from Viking times when farmers passed a horn of mead around the table and everyone drank with the understanding that no one should drink too much, lest they run out of brew before the mutton was served. In modern Swedish culture, the concept plays out as the perfect amount—of food, work, time, noise, emotion—and gives weight to the notion that balance is often achieved by taking the middle road.

USE: From the amount of sugar in your tea to the money shelled out for a comfy couch, use the word lagom to describe any fair decision made with moderation and mindfulness. As an adjective, it defines berries that are ripe for picking, coffee that's served at the ideal temperature and the moment your package arrives just in time for Christmas.

WORDS
ADRIENNE MATEI

Sense in Symmetry

*From radial swirls to
mirror images, the natural
world often shows that
there's beauty in balance.*

Mirror balance and algorithmic precision may sound like human fabrications, but taking a closer look at the circular swirl of a sunflower or the intricate Fibonacci sequence of a pinecone shows that nature is the original master of symmetry. Whether we're conscious of it or not, the designs we create often emulate the precise patterns we perceive in the natural world.

Many species of plants and animals share this distinct aesthetic feature (sea sponges are an exception; they do their own thing), and symmetry even extends into the cosmos: Astronomers have observed that the Milky Way galaxy is a perfect mirror image of itself, and it also exhibits a logarithmic spiral similar to a nautilus shell.

Applied to human design, symmetry provides a sense of aesthetic cohesion. British designer Barry Jackson was inspired by a beehive's versatile hexagons to create his inventive Hivehaus living units—prefabricated modular rooms ready to be conjoined into sleek and sustainable housing. In film, symmetry has the power to calm, such as Wes Anderson's perfectly balanced opening credits sequences. It appears in music: Tintinnabuli, Estonian maestro Arvo Pärt's compositional style, is based on the mathematical progression of symmetric structures that result in algorithmic symphonies. Even poems are made resonant by their measured syllabic meter, such as the iambic pentameter often learned in high school Shakespearean literature classes.

Catalan architect Antoni Gaudí believed that "nothing is art if it does not come from nature." He recognized that the natural world is rarely flawless and included purposeful imperfections in his designs: His knobby support beams simulate twisted tree trunks and his canopy ceilings replicate the marvels of organic engineering. These irregular natural details make his structures feel more, well, *natural*.

Likewise, unique touches of asymmetry endear us to our mates. Studies have shown a cross-cultural bias toward facial symmetry, yet we have a soft spot for crooked smiles, bumpy noses and beauty marks—an ironic term for what purists may consider facial blights. Despite surface appearances, nature is rarely mathematically perfect; it's the little quirks within it that convey authenticity, and reflecting these abnormalities in our own designs can keep things from striking us as unnaturally unsettling. (Think of *The Shining*'s geometrically patterned hallway carpets, for example.)

The irony of symmetry is that a bit of discord enhances rather than compromises its beauty. Contingent on elements of order and variance, both natural and constructed symmetry give us the feeling that all is well and demonstrate how deeply satisfying design can be when it is (almost) perfect.

SENSE IN SYMMETRY: Diamond by Bloomingville; round box by Bolia; candle holder by Menu; wooden shapes by HAY.

WORDS
MARGARET EVERTON

The Why
of the Storm

———

Where do the best ideas come from? Should we
surround ourselves with like minds, or does seclusion
breed the most creativity? We delve into the debate
about which conditions create the perfect brainstorm.

The word *brainstorm* hasn't always referred to some abrupt surge of insight. In fact, before the 20th century, it meant a brief malfunction of the mind—a "violent transient fit of insanity," as one dictionary definition goes. While the word has now shifted to describe the beginning stages of the creative process, the effort of coming up with a great idea can leave us feeling just as psychotic.

The term was popularized as a creative tactic when ad man Alex Osborn wrote about brainstorming in his 1948 book, *Your Creative Power*. People using his model began to think of ideation as a group effort, yet history is teeming with innovators who have worked best when alone. While we still may debate if group or individual brainstorming reigns supreme, there's no question that designing *how* we think can improve the quality of *what* we think.

Brainstorming is considered to be the divergent, volatile step of the creative process that values quantity over quality—its purpose being to get as many ideas as possible into the atmosphere without criticism. During this mental process, associative links run wild and collide, and our capacity to have a novel idea depends on our ability to blend old elements in new contexts. Despite the nonsense that may fill our pages, the aim is to encourage ideas to flow like rain.

Group brainstorms should encourage equal participation and off-the-cuff thinking. The velocity of impassioned people building on each other's ideas has resulted in manifestos, movements and revolutions (as well as objects such as the computer mouse and the Ferris wheel). The motion picture machine came about after photographer Eadweard Muybridge and phonograph inventor

Thomas Edison hung out. The Age of Enlightenment began gaining momentum when highly caffeinated philosophers chatted in coffee houses. And as one legend goes, the Reuben sandwich was created when hungry grocers played late-night poker in Omaha, Nebraska.

A study in *Scientific American* shows that the kind of social and intellectual diversity we experience at work enhances creativity. Instead of surrounding ourselves with like-minded people who share similar intellectual and cultural backgrounds, being exposed to a variety of personalities and disciplines can change how we think. Take Building 20 at MIT for example, where assorted faculty who knew nothing about each other's disciplines were crammed together in a temporary work space during World War II. The random overlap of knowledge bred profound innovations like the radar, the microwave, the first video game, Bose speakers and Noam Chomsky's structural take on linguistics, which was drawn from his casual exposure to computer science and biology. Simple logic suggests that the more distinct minds you can bring together to interact, the more unique combinations they will yield.

The slight stress that might arise as we drink coffee and scribble on butcher paper with our colleagues can bring out our creativity. Coming up with good ideas on the fly can quiet our minds' executive functions and activate the frontal lobes of the brain—it has been shown to light up an MRI in a pattern identical to a jazz trumpeter riffing, a dancer improvising or a rapper freestyling. The application of just enough social pressure can turn off our internal editor and give our creativity momentum.

ILLUSTRATION: KATRIN COETZER

But group brainstorming can also waste our time. Creativity is a highly individualized phenomenon that needs isolation when put to more complex tasks. In 1958, researchers at Yale University tested Osborn's brainstorming method by gathering one set of groups and another set of individuals and asking each to solve creative puzzles—and the solitary students came up with twice as many solutions. "Down with committees," once wrote advertising legend David Ogilvy, having observed for years how copywriters "dawdle about in brainstorming sessions and other forms of wheel-spinning" before getting to the task of actually writing.

He wasn't the only one to see deficiencies in bagel-fueled, time-eroding meetings. Studies have shown that the wrong kind of groups can stifle creativity. A study at Carnegie Mellon University shows that even one noisy or judgmental contributor can throw off the intelligence and confidence of an entire team. We've all felt stifled by a creative hijacker at some point—the team member who talks over us, the co-worker who spaces out at inopportune moments, the boss who scoffs at others' suggestions. In an effort to keep the peace and avoid ridicule, we might find ourselves striving for unanimity instead of searching for unique solutions.

The act of creating can be awkward and unglamorous, and sharing it can be like sheepishly revealing the contents of our bathroom medicine cabinet. Working on creative problems in privacy gives us space to explore the most seemingly stupid or silly notions without an audience. Science fiction writer Isaac Asimov wrote that for every good idea we have, there are countless others we don't want to display, and that the "presence of others can only inhibit this process, since creation is embarrassing." When we are free from social pressure and self-censorship, we often create more confidently.

But solo thinking doesn't have to mean sitting listlessly alone at our desk with a notepad. While we might want to power through a problem, neuropsychology shows that spending time doing pleasant, rote activities like doodling can help the brain work even more effectively. We need facts and knowledge to create new ideas, but we also need time and mental space to let our minds make the connections between them. Counterintuitive as it might feel, balancing intense concentration with downtime can invite a passive clarity that allows the finest ideas to form. Picasso conceived Cubism while lingering over African tribal masks in a Paris museum, author Alice Munro thought up stories while tending to her young children, and Mozart composed during carriage rides and sleepless nights, recognizing that "it is on such occasions that my ideas flow best and most abundantly." It's hard to imagine these three luminaries blocking off an hour to spar and problem-solve with co-workers.

In the end, we can diplomatically give both group and individual brainstorming a place in the creative process, using them to symbiotically bring out our best ideas. Our creative history is filled with innovators who both thought on their own *and* interlocked with other minds to launch cultural shakedowns. We can tackle tough questions in solitude and then come together to improve our notions. The hope is that through all this rumbling and storming, we will be ready when lightning strikes.

THE NATURE OF DESIRABILITY: Wooden items and cork cone by HAY; bottle by Menu; vase by Bolia; boxes by ferm LIVING.

The Nature
of Desirability

———

*The head of Harvard's Desirability Lab
examines what consumers like and why
so designers can create products that
hit the sweet spot.*

It's human nature to want things, but have you ever wondered why some objects or products affect you more than others? Dr. Beth Altringer, a professor at Harvard University's Graduate School of Design, has dedicated her life's work to that question. Her research focuses on what makes some designs more desirable than others, and she also founded the Desirability Lab, a think tank that "combines psychological research and hands-on design" to help creative innovators design products and services that will change lives. She gives us some insight into what people really want, even if they don't realize it.

WHAT PURPOSE DOES DESIRABILITY SERVE?

At its core, desirability is about both contextual and emotional decision making. We have intuitive and deliberate ways of thinking that help us survive and make sense of the world. In order to get it right, you need to develop ways to assess desire within context and to account for subjectivity. In terms of primal instinct, we have to make sense of our environment so we can assess threat and make decisions about how we spend our time.

WHY SHOULD WE BE INTERESTED IN LEARNING MORE ABOUT THE PSYCHOLOGY OF DESIRE?

Because we're influenced by desires whether we're deliberate about it or not. Developing a lens for desirability helps us to design better products, services and decision-making environments. It also helps us resist persuasive campaigns that aren't in our best interests. My goal is two-fold—to educate designers to create better products and services, and to educate individual decision makers to take a more active role in their decisions about what products and services enter their lives.

WHAT'S THE BIGGEST MISCONCEPTION WE HOLD ABOUT WHAT MAKES SOMETHING DESIRABLE OR NOT?

The most common misconception I see is the assumption that other people will like what we like. It's basically confirmation bias: "This is really cool, therefore everyone will think the same." This is a very human tendency, and while it's quite useful in many ways, it's also high-risk. It's important to implement mechanisms that slow down decision making and to develop a checks-and-balances system for your design process where you have some openness in your feedback.

WHAT SURPRISING OR UNEXPECTED DISCOVERIES HAVE YOU MADE?

That what we notice is often replicated in what we make. I feel like it's a dialogue of creation and consumption—we're kind of figuring out who we are through the artifacts that we bring into our lives. I've developed this habit of noticing and analyzing what students find desirable and undesirable in their world; I can see the conversation they're trying to have with the world through what they create and consume. We tend to think of these things separately, but looking at it as a dialogue helps us figure out who we are. It's fascinating and quite empowering when people embrace it. Until you understand how a product figures into people's lives in a really delightful way, you haven't truly figured out its design.

WHAT IS CREATIVITY?

There are different levels of creativity—researchers describe it as the little C, middle C and big C of creativity. The little version is putting coconut milk in your coffee—that's a little bit of creativity, and we all do that. The middle C is something in your job that you're doing that's unusual but noticeably creative. The big C is the game-changing creativity often seen in the media. Being creative is part of being human, and we're all doing it all the time.

HOW CAN PEOPLE APPLY THE NATURE OF DESIRABILITY TO HELP WITH CREATIVE PROBLEM SOLVING?

If you do one thing, develop the habit of noticing and analyzing the details of the world around you. What do you like and what don't you like, and why? The important thing is taking the time and committing to yourself. If you can find those patterns then you can develop your career around those patterns, because you probably won't get tired of those core themes.

The Lunch Box: Geometric Snacks

Take one cut-out cracker recipe, stack on different-shaped toppings and snack on these tessellated grown-up building blocks.

MAKES ABOUT 4 DOZEN

FOR THE ROSEMARY-RYE CRACKERS

1 cup/130 grams unbleached
   all-purpose flour, plus more
   for dusting
1 cup/140 grams rye flour
   (light or dark)
1 tablespoon fresh rosemary, chopped
1 teaspoon fine sea salt
¼ cup/60 milliliters extra-virgin
   olive oil, plus more for greasing
2 tablespoons honey
⅓ to ½ cup/75 to 120 milliliters water

Whisk together the all-purpose flour, rye flour, rosemary and salt in a large bowl. Drizzle in the olive oil and honey. Using a pastry cutter or fork, cut the wet ingredients into the flour mixture until no pieces are larger than small peas. While stirring, slowly drizzle in just enough water to form moist clumps of dough. Turn the dough out onto a lightly floured countertop and briefly knead it together to form a smooth ball. Cut the dough into 2 equal portions and shape each into a square or disk, depending on the shape of the crackers you plan to make. (A square for squares or triangles or a disk for rounds.) Wrap them in plastic wrap and let rest at room temperature for 20 to 30 minutes.

Preheat the oven to 375°F/190°C. Lightly grease 2 large baking sheets.

Place 1 portion of dough between 2 sheets of waxed or parchment paper and use a rolling pin to roll out to a thickness of about ⅛ inch/3 millimeters. Cut out 2 inch/5 centimeter squares or triangles—to get straight edges, use a ruler and a pastry wheel or pizza cutter. For circles, use a similar size cookie or biscuit cutter. Arrange them on one of the prepared baking sheets. Repeat with the second portion of dough, filling up the other baking sheet. Prick each cracker with a fork 2 or 3 times. Bake until the edges are golden brown, 12 to 15 minutes, rotating the pans in the oven halfway through. Transfer to a wire rack to cool and crisp. The crackers can be stored in an airtight container for up to 1 week.

STACK 1: SQUARE CRACKER
Slice of cured chorizo
Triangular slice of mango
Cube of manchego cheese

STACK 2: ROUND CRACKER
Half-moon slice of radish
Triangular slice of feta cheese
Pitted olive

STACK 3: TRIANGULAR CRACKER
Round slice of cucumber
Slice of hard-cooked egg
Cylindrical roll of salmon gravlax

STACK 4: ROUND CRACKER
Square slice of gorgonzola cheese
Half-moon slice of pickled beet
Mandarin orange wedge

STACK 5: TRIANGULAR CRACKER
Dried apricot
Roasted hazelnut
Rectangular section of celery filled with
   1 teaspoon honey butter
    (make using 4 tablespoons salted butter
    whipped with 1 tablespoon honey)

STACK 6: SQUARE CRACKER
Triangular slice of quince paste
Pistachio–goat cheese truffle
   (small ball of fresh goat cheese rolled
   in roasted and chopped pistachios)

PHOTOGRAPH: ANDERS SCHØNNEMANN; FOOD STYLING: MIKKEL KARSTAD; PROP STYLING: SIDSEL RUDOLPH

Nikolaj &
Mathias Mentze

―――

*As twin brothers and business partners,
this Danish design duo has learned to toe
the line between combining complementary
aesthetics and maintaining individuality.*

Growing up, Nikolaj and Mathias Mentze desperately wanted to be different from each other. The twins tried to carve their creative life paths separately—Nikolaj as a designer and Mathias as an architect—but they soon gave in to the inevitable. Following a few joint projects with Danish companies Bang & Olufsen and Kvadrat, they recently rejoined forces to cofound Studio 0405, a combined creative practice named after their birth date. We asked the brothers about what their shared upbringing has taught them about collaborative design.

WHAT KIND OF RELATIONSHIP DID YOU TWO HAVE WHEN YOU WERE GROWING UP?

Nikolaj (left): We come from a pretty cultural family: Our grandparents were movie directors and art critics, our father is a photographer and our mother is a journalist. As kids, we would build tree houses in our garden and make small cars out of wooden boxes and race them around, but I don't think either of us thought we'd end up working together.

Mathias (right): When you grow up being twins, you're constantly compared to one another. For the majority of our lives, this led to us trying to be as unlike each other as possible and creating our own very distinct identities. But every time we've gone in different directions, we've ended up in more or less the same place.

HOW HAS YOUR TWIN-DOM AFFECTED YOUR DESIGN PRACTICE?

Mathias: It's weird when people can't tell the difference between the two of us, since we don't look alike at all. Even though I think we're the most dissimilar set of twins you could imagine, we have a common aesthetic.

Nikolaj: Yes, we're pretty alike in taste, but having different design backgrounds makes our view on things different. However, if we always knew exactly what the other one was thinking without having to say anything, then that would be really practical...

WHAT PARTS OF YOUR PERSONALITY CAN WE SEE IN YOUR DESIGNS?

Nikolaj: My designs have a contrast between a clear, simple idea and something more complex, whether that's in the material or the sculpturality of the form. I also like things that have a temporal element, such as a surface that changes over time.

Mathias: I'm passionately interested in art—I look at and read about it every day. There's so much inspiration to be drawn from it, both in contemporary art and from art history, and my ideas for a new project will often come from a work of art that I admire.

WHAT IS THE DIFFERENCE BETWEEN DESIGN AND ART?

Nikolaj: Today the line between art, architecture and design is a lot more fluid. Artists explore the potential in design and vice versa—and I think that's positive for both parties.

HOW CAN DESIGN IMPROVE OUR QUALITY OF LIFE?

Mathias: I started designing out of a personal need to be surrounded by things I like. We are surrounded by design—everything is design. I think design and architecture work best when they have a strong connection to their context: The proportions of a room or the materials in a door handle can have a big impact on how we live in a certain space. It's important to look back and have a sense of where ideas come from and then try to make them relevant to today. Design is a continuous evolution of things or a conversation about what's relevant in our time and, ultimately, in the future.

WHAT DO YOU LIKE TO DO WHEN YOU'RE NOT WORKING? WHAT'S THE DANISH IDEA OF DOWNTIME?

Mathias: If I get the chance, I'd rather get out of town—go to a cabin in the countryside, take a walk along the coast or light a fire in the fireplace. Both of us have also always enjoyed cooking—I love preserving fruits and vegetables during fall.

Nikolaj: Mathias makes a mean quince marmalade!

PHOTOGRAPH: CHRISTIAN FRIIS

Kai Avent-deLeon

———

*Like her mother and grandmother before her,
this fashion boutique owner has used grassroots
innovation—and a dose of caffeine—to cultivate
community in her native Brooklyn.*

With stints at esteemed fashion houses such as Chanel under her belt, Kai Avent-deLeon could've gone anywhere. But instead of being tempted by the bright lights of Manhattan, she decided to return to her native neighborhood in Brooklyn to open up her own fashion boutique—Sincerely, Tommy. Also equal parts coffee shop, art gallery, event space and community center, its location on a residential street in Bedford-Stuyvesant (Bed-Stuy) has connected previously separate communities. As a third-generation business owner in the area, Kai draws from her family's heritage to form a framework for future local creatives.

HOW HAVE YOU TRIED TO ENGAGE THE LOCALS OF BED-STUY?

It was really important for me to start a conversation. I wanted to create a place that was about more than just buying something, so the coffee counter serves as an interactive area of the store. We have our core customers who come in every day to get a coffee and hang out and talk with the staff. There's always some sort of dialogue—often about cultural or social issues going on right now—and I love to see those conversations happening.

WHAT EFFECT HAS THE STORE HAD ON THE NEIGHBORHOOD?

The store has created its own kind of community, but we also belong to a bigger community that's already been established in this neighborhood. It's really nice to see how the two groups engage with one another when we have events. I definitely think there's a need for some sort of inspiration or encouragement to do something positive, because I don't see a lot of that being pushed around here to the kids just hanging out on the stoop. The message of the store is conveyed to the young people in this neighborhood—do what you're passionate about, be good about it, and work hard.

HOW HAS YOUR FAMILY INFLUENCED YOUR CAREER?

Oh, they've played a huge role. My grandmother took a leap of faith in purchasing some property in Bed-Stuy back when it was really dangerous and she was discouraged to do so, and then my mom followed in her footsteps by opening a vegan restaurant here in 2004 before the whole vegan trend had really hit. My dad also does work with low-income homes in the neighborhood. They've always been pioneers, and I think that I inevitably had it in me to just do something and take a risk. They're so supportive—even up to this day, they just pop in to see if they can help. They're my biggest fans.

WHAT HAVE YOUR MOTHER AND GRANDMOTHER TAUGHT YOU?

They're both very stylish women, so I've definitely gained my love of fashion from them. My grandmother is probably the sweetest woman I've ever met and puts people before herself, but my mom's kind of the opposite—stern and very honest—so it's a good balance. My mom always preaches that you have to put your health first. She's always making sure that I'm not on the computer until 3 a.m. and not working with it sitting on my lap—all those little things to make sure I'm taking care of myself. I also do the things that I don't enjoy first, as it makes it a lot easier to flow into everything else I would rather be doing.

HOW DOES THE STORE SUPPORT YOUNG DESIGNERS?

I felt that so many of my favorite stores in New York were just carrying the same brands, so I thought I'd do something different. I seek out young talents who either don't have the resources to create a website or they can't afford a booth at a trade show. I've definitely taken on a kind of mentor role with some of the local designers I work with—they're passionate about their lines and about creating something, but sometimes they don't understand the other things that go into it, whether it's production or quality control.

WHAT IS THE KEY TO OPENING A STORE THAT SUCCESSFULLY PARTICIPATES IN A NEIGHBORHOOD'S ECOSYSTEM?

You have to look at the bigger picture. I asked myself, "How can I make a change in my community?" Maybe I can't change the world and maybe this won't go beyond Bed-Stuy, but if it takes a village, then what positive contribution can I make? Not everyone might understand the store, but the idea of knowing that someone from this neighborhood decided to stay here to open something of value is really important.

PHOTOGRAPH: ZOLTAN TOMBOR

Max Lamb

Whether designing a chair, a teaspoon or a shop's interior, this British industrial designer takes the concept of community into his own hands.

The user's experience is not the only element that's essential to the success of Max Lamb's work: It's just as important to consider how each product will affect the community as a whole, whether that's an entire neighborhood or simply the folk who you share a dinner table with. For his ongoing project, *Exercises in Seating*, Max has created dozens of chairs as a way to explore new materials and production processes (while feeding his endless fascination with forms of seating). His book of the same name documents the story behind each piece, from technical information on growing nanocrystalline copper to anecdotes of salvaging an ash tree from his grandfather's farm in Yorkshire. He speaks about how handcrafted objects can enrich our daily lives and how design can help strengthen our relationships with those around us.

My wife, Gemma, and I recently moved into our new home, which is also our studio. When we were renovating, I set myself a one-mile radius from our postal code and only employed people who were living and working on our doorstep. It was important for me to get to know people, to get to know the community and to support local trade rather than a multinational company that has a nice fancy website. Instead, I found my tradespeople using the Yellow Pages.

After we'd renovated and transformed the building—it had previously been a mosque for 20 years—we moved into a part of the city that we were completely unfamiliar with. That kind of raised a lot of surprises and questions for us: Who were we? And what gave us the right to suddenly move into this area and call it home? Other than hiring local tradespeople to help us renovate, we hadn't been born and raised in or even contributed to the community as of yet.

Then recently a woman who lives around the corner from us was trying to arrange a street party, so we helped her plan it with a number of other residents. We met in the local pub and put together a checklist of all the things that we could do and who we should be inviting. We had the street blocked off by the local council so that all the children could play in the roads, and everybody was assigned a role. Being the furniture designer, I produced all the tables—they were kind of ad-hoc assemblies of raw materials that I had kicking around in my workshop with clamps to hold everything in place.

We transformed the entire street. It was quite amazing to see how many people came from one street yet from all different walks of life, cultures, parts of the world and all with different occupations and skills of trade. Yet we all came together and contributed something. It was really a special occasion.

For me, that's kind of design in a way. It was a hugely creative process because we had to make do with no budget—we all had to contribute something we already had and use our imaginations to produce something to create this festival atmosphere. Design plays a part in the creation of that atmosphere and that sense of community.

Previous spread: Inspired by childhood trips to the beach, Max sculpted these hexagonal and triangular stools using a primitive sand casting technique that involves pouring molten pewter into a hand-carved mold in the sand. They were part of his *Exercises in Seating* exhibition.

"My work is always about a fundamental gathering of people— this could be classified as my community."

I make work not for myself but for other people. It's a bit of an insular process of creativity as I'm not in communication with the end user, the viewers or the community—whoever they are—but I'm still very much a part of the dialogue with them, whether it's for a private commission, an individual customer or a company. I'm currently working on a project for a British manufacturer of wooden furniture called Benchmark, which was founded by Terence Conran.

My work is always about a fundamental gathering of people—this could be classified as my community. Whether in the fashion, interior or graphic design industry, there's always quite a strong sense of community: We're typically very sociable people who like to talk and share ideas, and that's true of my practice too.

Gemma and I are proper little collectors. We love smaller artifacts. I think I probably began my gathering habit more focused on furniture. I do have a slight focus on chairs, so we have 12 chairs around our dining table and they're all different. I've always been fascinated with furniture, and it was almost like a research process of bringing all these wonderful examples of both historic and contemporary design into my home and my world. They feed into my practice and help me understand geometry, ergonomics, construction and materials.

But we can only bring so many chairs into one house, so we started looking at smaller objects. We are lovers of the kitchen and eating, and Gemma especially enjoys the process of cooking, which is very generous and community-driven—it's nourishing in more than one sense of the word.

So we love to collect kitchen paraphernalia and have a rather ridiculous quantity of it, specifically ceramics, pottery, crockery and the utensils we use to cook with, eat from and serve food on. We especially collect studio ceramics and pottery from the UK, primarily Cornwall, but also Japanese and other Asian pottery. We collect these things because we use them—some of them sit on our windowsills and shelves, but they're constantly rotating on a regular basis so that they're all being used. It gives such a warm feeling to the process of eating.

We love having objects that are made by hand by a real human being. We have plates made by Bernard Leach—maybe not by Bernard himself, but by one of his apprentices— and they're each different with a unique signature and fingerprint. So you have 12 people around your dining table, sitting in different chairs, all eating off plates made in one go by one pottery and fired in the same kiln, yet they all sort of have their own unique characteristics.

Products are no longer being made locally for local consumption and use—this is for the worse, in many senses, but for the better in others too. We have ended up with an incredibly refined visual language for products based almost solely on how they're made and what they're made of—a very rational beauty has evolved and emerged.

However, as with anything, it's human nature to get tired and bored and want change. After all, we're organic creatures, aren't we? So we start to crave other things, and I think that's where we've really started to change as producers and consumers in the last 15 years. There are always many overlapping layers, directions and tastes, but at least in the community I know, belong to and communicate with, there is a growing desire for individual personality and celebrating that individuality. And in parallel, there's a growing population with the ability to provide that.

In the rise of the homemade, the handmade, the craft-made and the self-made— whatever you want to call it—there's this revival of the individual and the idea of creating a product that satisfies a particular use or user rather than the global population. In many cases, I think that's why we're returning to old processes, materials and methods of production. But we're also generating new ones that allow a similar approach to small-batch local productions—we're generating a new language and a new form of beauty in itself.

Design

WORDS
AVI FRIEDMAN

PHOTOGRAPHS
ANDERS SCHØNNEMANN

A VIEW FROM THE PORCH

The shapes and sizes of our homes are changing, and society along with it. As the author of more than a dozen books on the intersection of architecture and domestic life, architect and professor Avi Friedman has come to make sense of a new era of household realities. In this edited excerpt from his latest book, A View From the Porch (Véhicule Press, 2015), he considers how social patterns are altering the designs of our homes and the ways we live in them.

"Fridges should be manufactured with expandable doors," my wife suggested one evening as she tried to affix a note with a magnet to the crowded surface of our refrigerator. As two very busy academics with two active teenagers, managing time in our home required an almost military efficiency. My children are grown-up now and have their own places, but back then we were endlessly trying to catch up with one another's schedules: Driving the kids to school, after-school sports and social activities, respecting community and social obligations, attending medical appointments and parent-teacher interviews, keeping up with household chores like grocery shopping and laundry pickup—altogether, it didn't seem to leave time for much else.

Today's increasing pressure on the family schedule is a result of several factors, among which is, paradoxically, the home itself. The gradual expansion in the size of homes and their amenities in the 1970s drove their prices up and necessitated two incomes for their purchase and maintenance. The subsequent return of women to the labor force restructured household responsibilities and priorities. With both parents working, the family's basic daily chores now had to be compressed into the weekend and a smaller number of weekday hours—Mom or Dad were simply not there full time to look after household necessities. Every time slot before the beginning and after the end of a workday had to be taken advantage of. And the internet made it even more tempting to put aside family responsibilities and focus on work.

Eventually, I realized that I was whisking through some of life's events too quickly. I began to regard time as a commodity, and I tried to find answers within the realm of my profession—design—to the challenges I faced at home.

So how does one make use of the few precious minutes that we have to spare for a family get-together during the day? We can start by altering family behavior, reshaping priorities and placing human relations at the top of the list. And proper design can help.

It begins by establishing comfortable spaces in which family members can sit together. For example, once it's been decided that breakfast together is important, a cozy dining area adjacent to the kitchen is conducive to pleasant talks about the coming day. Having it properly lit with a serving counter nearby so that everyone can remain seated can make a difference. In the very same space, dinner can take place to the sound of soft music. Alternatively, families can revive their old, forgotten dining room and eat there daily.

The home's decor and accessories can also be made to foster strong family relations by serving as a reminder of roots and times past. As I make my way through rooms, I walk through time. It's not a house I'm traversing, but a life: the recorded memory of moments, days and years of the people who live there. When I began to design, I concluded that homes are as much about memories and aspirations as they are about walls and shades of paint.

"The home's decor and accessories can be made to foster strong family relations by serving as a reminder of roots and times past."

Homes are the backdrops of our lives. When children go out into the world, perhaps to form their own families, they can always turn back to that collection of memorable images and use them to build their own homes.

Speculative builders refer to homes as *product*. Whereas homebuyers see their lives unfolding in residences, builders have a nearer horizon: They have to sell and build quickly and move on to the next project. Handing over the keys to a buyer is their ultimate goal. A model home—the showcase of a new development, like a new model in a car dealership—must therefore look good. It ought to draw a "Wow," make an unsure buyer fall in love at first sight and edge out the competition across the street. A hotel-size kitchen with stainless-steel appliances will be an anchor; a spacious marble-tiled bathroom with trendy fixtures and a Jacuzzi will be an attention grabber. It's all a question of first impressions.

Despite my experience working with builders, I'm often uneasy when I have to present my design to one. I know their critique will be harsh and thorough. The success or failure of their investment, I feel, rests on the shoulders of my design. Throughout our discussion, the ultimate user of the design—the homeowner—is faceless and referred to as a client.

I parked my car near a newly constructed house in a barren development and stepped into a very cold January afternoon. It was a Friday, and I could tell that the builder's office receptionist was eager to end the week. The months of January and February are traditionally the busy season in the home-building business in North America, since people tend to buy houses for summer occupancy. The number of sales during these months determines the year's overall activity. So designs are rushed, finalized and made ready for buyers to see and purchase.

From inside the office I could hear one end of a heated telephone conversation. It sounded as if Jack, the builder, was in the midst of an argument with his banker

about interest he was being charged on a line of credit. He wasn't likely to be in a good mood when he saw me.

The call finally ended. Jack stepped out to instruct his secretary, noticed me, and asked me to come in. He was an experienced builder who built primarily for the move-up market—those who had sold their first small house and were buying a bigger one. He referred to his homes as Buicks: large, comfortable, yet not too expensive. This time though, he was about to start a housing development made up of entry-level homes that would appeal to young couples with a modest income. I'd been recognized for my expertise in designing affordable housing, which Jack wanted me to apply to this project.

After a brief greeting, Jack cleared his wide desk as he pointed to my roll of drawings and said, "Let's see what you have for me today." I unrolled the plans, and began to describe the layout of the two-story-plus-basement townhouse I'd designed. I animated my description by walking him through the unbuilt home as if he were a visitor. He listened to my explanation, cutting me off at times when he thought I'd taken too long. It felt as if his mind was still in conversation with his banker.

"What's the unit's overall area?" he asked. I told him. He pulled out a smartphone from his pocket and punched in some numbers. "Too expensive," he said. "I'll have trouble selling such a product in this site."

That took the wind out of my sails—I'd been hoping to get his approval so that I could prepare the construction documents. Now I might have to begin my design all over again.

"What can we take out to make the home smaller?" he asked.

There was silence. Sitting there, mulling over the plans, we pondered which functions we could do without. "I can shrink the kitchen and the main bathroom a bit," I proposed.

"You're kidding. Kitchens and bathrooms are my real-estate agents," he said.

"I can reduce the parents' bedroom area," I offered.

"The parents are paying for this home. Don't start with them," Jack responded quickly. "Maybe you can shrink the living room and knock off the dining room," he suggested after a moment of silence. "In our home," he continued, "hardly anyone ever sits in the living room, and the dining room is never used."

"What about holidays and family gatherings?" I asked.

"What's the point of keeping valuable space for events that take place only once or twice a year?" Jack said, dismissing my argument. He glanced at his watch and suggested that I reconsider my design and we meet the following week.

On the drive back to my office, I reflected on Jack's comments about the living and dining rooms and his suggestion to do without them. Are these rooms really needed?

New lifestyle trends have shifted traditional family schedules, and for many people today, it's hard to find time for a formal meal in the dining room on a weeknight. Setting the table, carrying the food there, taking time to discuss the day's events, cleaning up and moving to the living room for coffee and dessert while listening to music—that all seems like an evening from a long-gone era.

In his book *A History of Domestic Space*, Peter Ward points out that the living room, which was also called a parlor, salon, sitting room or front room, was once the place where the family met acquaintances and presented itself to the outside world. It was the home's most public space. This was also the room in which a family would display their material accomplishments and treasured mementos. Paintings, family heirlooms, silverware and photos were hung on walls and put in glass cases. According to Peter Ward, a piano was also common in middle-class homes in Europe and North America: It was a mark of culture and a signal of wealth. Musical and vocal talents were highly valued, and playing for guests

was part of formal hospitality. Extended family members or visitors would gather after dinner to chat, play cards and listen to music played on the piano.

The dining room likewise used to serve a formal function. Its seating arrangements signified the family's hierarchy; the two heads of table had more comfortable chairs than the ones alongside. In the 1960s, family dinners provided an important social function, creating a formal setting for family exchange, reflection on the day's events and a forum for a get-together. More than just a room to house the table and chairs, the dining room became a bonding place. Families would discuss—or often debate (this being the '60s)—important matters before Dad handed over the car keys to a teenager of driving age after dessert. At family gatherings, guests would continue to sit long after dinner ended to talk, giggle over photos or simply catch up with the events of each other's lives.

The mid-1980s saw families and lifestyles transform. Households became smaller and children grew up. It became hard to fill up the empty chairs around the Baby Boomers' tables, and thus the dining room's decline began. Its former glory was restored only a few times a year, its charm being revisited on Thanksgiving, Christmas and other special occasions.

The use of space at home has also become gradually more decentralized. Do we really need to retain a separate room for an occasion that may occur only once or twice a year? Shouldn't the current trends dictate a new priority list in how homes are used? In many homes today, the dining room has taken on new roles: kids use the large table surface to do homework; Mom or Dad sets up a computer on the corner to run a freelance business; receipts and bills litter the table at tax time. With the increase in the number and nature of tasks that a modern family has to perform, the dining room often becomes, at least temporarily, a substitute for a study.

The living room has experienced a similar fate with the rise of informality.

—

"Homes are as much about memories and aspirations as they are about walls and shades of paint."

A regular weekday or weekend visit by extended family or acquaintances became a rarity. As the price of sound systems and televisions went down, they appeared in several rooms, and no longer did the family need to gather in the living room for entertainment.

The composition of a typical household has also changed. Families made up of stay-at-home mom, working dad and two or three kids no longer dominate the demographic pie chart. The share of what demographers call "non-traditional" families in the population has grown. There are more single-parent families, more same-sex couples with or without children and more singles than there used to be a decade or two ago.

In the future, with expected growth in apartment living and the shrinkage of the average household size in the city, small will dominate. The introduction of micro-units (less than 50 square meters [500 square feet]) in cities like New York, London and Vancouver marked the disappearance of the dining room and the slashing of the living space. In addition, coffeehouses styled to look like a living room with sofas and fireplaces have become the meeting place of choice for younger apartment dwellers.

Yet, living and dining rooms still play an important role in the lives of residents. They are as much social and cultural icons as they are functional spaces. As my conversation with Jack the builder demonstrated, both the social perception of and economic justification for a formal living or dining space is undergoing re-evaluation. But as current lifestyle trends result in greater family seclusion, it's important to have uniting symbols.

The dining room represents such a space. Whether it's once a week or several times a year, eating there can put people in a festive mood. Wearing our Sunday best and eating comfort food off the "good" dishes in a formal setting constitutes a ritual we should not abandon. On special occasions and holidays, it's the room where relatives from near and far

congregate. Like the best suits we don for special occasions and jewelry we wear once or twice a year, the dining room is a space to keep. And even when it's not being used, the formal setting, with the table in the middle and chairs all around, sends a clear message about the institution of family.

The living room should continue to play a similar role. After-dinner conversations in a relaxed setting—such as sitting in an armchair or on a sofa while listening to quiet background music—is a sign of civility we seem to have lost. Both living and dining rooms can be gathering places for families. The spaces could be transformed, perhaps, but their original purpose should remain intact: comfortable rooms that provide a transition between the world outside and within.

Back at the office, I unrolled my drawings again and thought about what Jack had said. I saw his point: too large a home would be too expensive and wouldn't sell. So I decided to shrink all the space equally but keep, albeit transformed, the living and dining rooms. Luckily, he saw my point.

With living rooms and dining rooms becoming less important, the kitchen has become the home's social space. The open-plan concept has taken on a new meaning and has turned the entire floor, or most of it, into one large area with several functions feeding into the kitchen. Kids' homework, home accounting, watching TV, entertaining friends and reading all take place in this once-humble space. Ironically, the preferred 21st-century home layout mirrors the ones of the settlers starting their lives in North America—the one-room house.

Turning the kitchen into the family's social center necessitated further upgrades in appearance. Manufacturers didn't miss a beat. They paid more attention to form and design, calling in top industrial designers to turn bulky appliances into design masterpieces. Clad in stainless-steel facings, black edges and digital readouts, appliances took on a slick personality.

Previous spread: A favorite feature in their kitchen is one you can't actually see: an Italian-style invisible plate rack that sits above the sink. "You put wet dishes inside a cupboard without a base so the water drains back to the sink," Isis says. "I love it." Their kitchen was designed by Marcante-Testa and produced by MateriaDesign.

Despite our reliance on ready-to-serve meals, homeowners have been willing to pay for the ability to prepare gourmet dinners at home on special occasions.

Blame it on our lifestyles, technology or plain consumerism, but society has changed and people's eating habits have changed as well. Many people have gradually disengaged from cooking their own food—the most human and potentially rewarding of tasks. Burgeoning frozen-food sections and the birth of the fast-food chains were testaments to the fact that North American households had shifted to convenience food. Few peel tomatoes to make Grandma's lasagna; instead we thaw a frozen meal and serve it in minutes. Even that American icon, the burger, is now sold frozen in a bun with condiments. Large, once-a-week shopping has also expanded pantry space. Frozen-food storage has required larger fridges, and a separate freezer in the basement has been added for long-term storage.

Ready-to-serve frozen food benefited from the invention of another appliance: the microwave oven. It was invented in 1946 by accident when Dr. Percy Spencer, an American, tested a radar-related tube called a magnetron. During one of the experiments, a candy bar in his pocket melted. Further testing made him realize the significance of his invention.

Information appliances have also expanded the home's time and space to allow occupants to be anywhere, any time. They have brought slices of activities into the home that used to be carried out in other places not so long ago: A bank, a library, and a travel agency are some of the establishments that we used to visit in person during daytime hours and that we can now access digitally from home. We can see and speak with strangers and loved ones, tour places anywhere in the world in real time and choose our preferred type of entertainment from the comfort of our sofas. Yet at the same time, to some degree, they've detached us from these places; we no longer need to patronize them in person.

In recent years, the layouts of homes have made them thoroughly public places. A great number of intimate and private places have been lost. The transformation took place when—in the name of style, convenience or space—functions were combined and the open-plan concept thrived. The space that has seen the greatest decline in intimacy is the bedroom, where a TV has become an indispensable feature. Quiet time for reading or conversation that was once part of the ritual of changing gears at the end of a hectic day is now filled with more digital or electronic appliances instead. By the same token, those appliances have also contributed to segregation within the home itself. Household members are now being engaged with more time-consuming tools. Time spent in face-to-face conversation seems to have diminished.

The telephone was the first appliance to open the home's communication avenue and alter home life. I wondered how the telephone, besides being a technological breakthrough, had affected domestic design since its introduction. How had it influenced community relations? What's next in the relationship between the home and those appliances?

When Alexander Graham Bell patented the telephone in 1876, he changed the nature of human interaction overnight. The ability to reach someone at once and carry on a live conversation over a wire rendered written messages sent by snail mail obsolete, to a certain degree. Instant communication was born and, along with it, instant exchange of news and ideas.

Like other great inventions that preceded and followed it, the telephone was first viewed with skepticism—early forecasters even argued that it would never take off since its initiators wouldn't be able to find enough single women between the ages of 16 and 20 to operate the manual switchboards. Only a few envisioned the effect that the telephone would eventually have on home design and life in the following century. When it was first introduced, the telephone was placed in

"Wireless technology and the introduction of smartphones have further blurred the line between the home and the world outside."

Right: A rack system created by OM Project and MateriaDesign runs through the house. The screens are perforated so that different rooms can still be seen while also creating the feeling of separate spaces.

"Like the best suits we don for special occasions and jewelry we wear once or twice a year, the dining room is a space to keep."

the hallway or the living room, close to the entrance. Given its sporadic use, it was initially enclosed within a cabinet. Only years later would it be hung on the wall and, later still, stand alone.

The ring of a telephone disturbed routine family activities and attracted immediate attention. People would gather around to find out who called and what the message was. Party lines meant that people could listen to their neighbors' private conversations. The telephone also marked the beginning of the blurring of the line between home and work in the modern era: In the years that followed, as services expanded, the same lines were used for homes and businesses, allowing people at home to receive after-hours calls directed to their offices.

The introduction of telephones also transformed the residential street and the front porch. Whereas face-to-face encounters had served as the main mode of communal social contact, chatting in person became less necessary when you could talk on the phone with a neighbor across the street or acquaintance across town.

Over the following decades, as telephone technology transformed from manual to automated switchboards and hardware and service costs went down, a telephone extension in other rooms appeared. Some people installed a second line, enabling household members, often teenagers, to conduct extended conversations from the privacy of their rooms. With these clear demarcations within the family, phone calls within the home turned from a public into a private affair.

Then in the 1950s, the installation of jacks throughout the house enabled people to talk on the phone while preparing dinner, watching TV or working on a school project. Cordless communication in the 1990s encouraged mobility from room to room. A person could now verify information or check a reference without saying, "I'll call you back."

Similar to the telephone—which has generated advantages at the same time as contributing to societal losses—

the introduction of computers brought the very same ambivalence. Just a few years after their introduction, they had a tremendous impact on the domestic realm.

The late 1990s saw great speculation about the relationship between the home and its environment in the digital age. The term *cocooning* was introduced, forecasting that relationships between the home and outside services would be handled mainly by computers. Forecasts turned out to be exaggerated, yet the basic infrastructure remained intact.

The location of computers in homes has also changed along with their increasing importance. They were first put in the basement when they were used for hobby or play, moved to the study when they became a sophisticated typewriter and relocated again to the children's bedroom desk when they became more versatile. They then turned mobile with the introduction of the laptop and Wi-Fi.

More than just a technological and communications breakthrough, the computer marked the start of the knowledge revolution. From the comfort of domestic spheres, it permitted access to huge stockpiles of data at an enormous speed. Wireless technology and the introduction of smartphones coupled with the proliferation of the World Wide Web widened this convenience, further blurring the line between the home and the world outside.

If the telephone reduced the need for face-to-face contact and contributed to the erosion of the front porch, computers and smartphones *became* the porch. In fact, they became the public square.

It is hard to predict what kind of digital devices will be invented and what their future effect on the domestic environment will be. However, we can rest assured that in the roller coaster of ongoing consumption, more is in store for us. If recently introduced gadgets are any indication of what is coming, we are in for an exciting ride, whether we like it or not.

"Even when it's not being used, the dining room sends a clear message about the institution of family."

Left: Formal and forgotten in many modern apartments, the dining area in Isis and Karel's home remains social by sharing space with the living room. On weekends, the family likes to use the two spaces to eat, debate, listen to music and play *belote*, their favorite card game.

IN CONVERSATION:

ILSE CRAWFORD & HUGO MACDONALD

———

It's one of design's chicken-and-egg questions: Is current home design changing the way we live, or is the way we live changing current home design? Ilse Crawford is one of Britain's most well-respected interior designers and centers her outlook around human relationships, and Hugo Macdonald is the former design editor of Monocle *and is currently writing a book for The School of Life called* How to Live in the City. *After reading the previous excerpt from Avi Friedman's* A View From the Porch, *we sat down with the interior design denizens behind StudioIlse to discuss some of the book's fundamental themes.*

How can we change the design of our homes to encourage us to slow down?

ILSE: Essentially, I think the process is two-pronged: On the one hand, a lot more thinking needs to go into physical space to make it friction-free. As designers, we need to think about it beforehand so it's almost intuitive once it reaches the user—all that planning and intelligence is implicit. At StudioIlse, we talk about making physical space more like the physical embodiment of human behavior—when we work on homes, we spend a lot of time looking, listening and watching how the residents actually occupy their existing spaces, and only after that do we come up with something we think is relevant. It goes way beyond thinking about how it looks—it's built around their needs.

That's one response to society's increasing speediness: making designs effective rather than efficient. We don't want to waste time trying to do things, find things and make things happen when they're completely unnecessary. At the same time, we don't want to live like machines: We want to feel "at home." We want to prioritize the unmeasurable stuff: things like atmosphere,

tactility, beauty and comfort. These qualities slow you down; they really embed your body in a place. We're tactile, sensorial, emotional beings, so it's important that we're living—properly *living*—in a space and not dashing through our days.

The other side of it is to create rituals and habits within the home. Those key moments in a day need more attention. When we invoke the Danish word *hygge* at the studio, we're talking about identifying tiny moments and making them important. That's because it's the combination of the tiny moments in a day that makes life matter, slows things down and connects you to other people.

How do you create a space for those rituals to flourish?

HUGO: It's about making room for them and not being too prescriptive in your approach to design. You want to create a framework to enable those rituals to take place. People need to have space to be able to inhabit their homes with their own lives.

ILSE: Yes, it's not about strictly saying, "Right, now it's time for your ritual!"

HUGO: We were looking at some interiors in a book recently, and it struck us how fixed they were. The pictures and rooms were beautiful, but when you dug into them and imagined how they might feel in reality, you got a sense that they were claustrophobic and that there was very little of yourself you could bring to them—every tiny thing had already been taken care of.

Actually leaving space for your own life and the serendipitous moments that happen minute by minute, hour by hour and day by day is crucial to creating room for slowing down—it's such an important thing to try and build into our lives. We're being invaded by technology to such an extent that we're sharing pictures from our pillows. The boundaries between public and private have all but disappeared, and a lack of privacy is invading our lives. I've stopped taking my phone and laptop into my bedroom, just to be able to switch off both literally and metaphorically and get to sleep. Technology development is hugely important—

ILSE: —as is the etiquette around it and making parameters where you're not defined by it. It's a set of tools—you exist independently of that.

HUGO: I think that technology and the way we live with it has fundamentally changed our perceptions of home and how we live in our homes. When you're looking at photos on social media, you see people's lives in the background of the pictures. It's fascinating and riveting, but at the same time you think, "Oh my goodness—I'm sharing so much more of my private life than I realized!" It's terrifying when you wonder, "What is private in my life, apart from what's inside my head?" For the millennial generation, re-establishing the boundaries of what makes a home "private" is very important, and I think we're going to start asking more of these questions going forward.

It's not just the information we're sharing ourselves but also the implicit information we're picking up from others. We used to linger over the dinner table for hours while catching up, but now when we sit down, we've already seen photos of our friends' trip to Italy and know that their brother has just started a new job. How do you see technology changing the way we interact socially?

ILSE: And you've also made up your mind about the social situation, which I think is interesting. It's not a discussion anymore—it's rather like talking about the news, where everybody has an opinion about a news story without ever really knowing what's going on.

HUGO: It's strange and rather alarming when you open your eyes and look at just how much we're being sucked into the technology we live with and how detached from the real experience we are.

ILSE: It's interesting how everything is connected. Collectively, I think there's this sense of the endless present—that the future seems so far away.

How is the meaning of home changing as technology and design change?

ILSE: The deep, psychological meaning we have for home is not discussed enough. We've commodified home to such a large extent in the last few decades, so it's not surprising that there's such a craving for that place of safety again—somewhere that you feel you belong, where you can be yourself. It's an important part of your well-being.

HUGO: And it's becoming harder to find. I speak to my parents a lot about the difficulty of being yourself in the modern world. They think I'm indulgent and I should have a stiff upper lip, but they've lived in the same house in the countryside for decades—city living is a different bag entirely. You need to carve out your own space in your urban environment. Finding space for yourself to just think and breathe is increasingly difficult, but we're all becoming more aware of how essential it is; thinking of home as a sanctuary is more vital than ever.

ILSE: Most animals have a home—it's a primal need, not an affectation. To be "homeless" is not just to be without a house; the feeling of vulnerability that goes with having no home is really profound.

The divide between public and private realms in the home is rapidly changing. We seem to have lost the parlor, which is where guests used to be entertained. Is this trend global?

ILSE: Some cultures still have those: Russians have many layers of the private sphere, which is quite Eastern in that respect. And South America still has the parlor: I'm married to a Colombian, and we're constantly going to see aunts in these rooms where the chairs are literally arranged around the walls and you're sitting there being scrutinized by 99 aunts and god-knows how many cousins... It's fascinating.

HUGO: We also no longer have specific functions for different rooms. This is by virtue of the fact that homes in cities are a lot smaller than they once were, so space now has to be multifunctional.

"Leaving space for the serendipitous moments
that happen minute by minute is crucial to
creating room for slowing down."

ILSE: Purpose-orientated rooms are a 19th-century construct. Before that, rooms were very multipurpose: If you look at medieval times, you would have dinner in the great hall where *everything* happened—and then the only other real space was your bedroom. Homes change in response to the times: Victorian homes are very structured because society suddenly became very structured, and they reflect that.

HUGO: I think of places where I've lived in London, and apart from the bathroom and maybe the bedroom, it's really been one-room living. And that's an amazing thing in itself: You see how furniture doubles up with its functions and also how you inhabit different parts of that room for different mental states. That area becomes imbued with that property.

ILSE: Maybe that's why habits and rituals are coming back up the scale—because it's part of the checks and balances. We can't have zones anymore for specific things, but we can draw attention to certain moments. I think they go hand in hand; though they seem like opposites, they're actually in partnership.

So you're saying that because we don't have physically private spaces to retreat to anymore, we're therefore seeking to uphold those little personal rituals elsewhere? How else is this mindset played out in a home's design?

ILSE: At the studio, we talk a lot about the six inches around you: Your experience of being in a space is often defined by your immediate surroundings much more than the space you can see beyond that.

It's quite fascinating, because the way that design has developed over the last few decades has been focused on the visual. If you go to a restaurant, your first impressions are often based on the way it looks, but your experience is actually defined not only by what you eat, but also by what you sit on and what you touch. It's also true in the home. We should be conscious of choosing things that affect the way we feel, such as the weight of a glass.

My other life involves being the head of the Department of Man and Well-Being at the Design Academy Eindhoven, and we have some intriguing projects. For example, we were recently looking at the glass: Can you design a happy glass, a sad glass, a glass that's supposed to make you excited? It's interesting to work out how you can consciously conjure up an emotional connection through a physical object, even though it's essentially the same item. Design has a lot of potential to really focus on intimate objects that can massively change your feelings. And if you can change your feelings, you can change your thoughts and vice versa.

HUGO: And the aesthetic is a distraction really, isn't it?

ILSE: Yes, aesthetics are just one part of many. The integration of all of design's properties is where it becomes really interesting: How is a product going to affect you?

There's so much information and inspiration out there that we're able to gather from different areas, which can make us feel like experts when we're not. How are our endless choices affecting us?

HUGO: I recently said to Ilse that I think people are less tolerant of bad function than ever before, partly because there's just so much choice: We can very quickly discard something that doesn't work for something that does. There's no excuse for something not to function properly. Aesthetics have been very important in the past, but today we need tools that work more than ever, ones that support us in our lives. It's only when everything functions equally that you make a decision based more on what an object looks like.

ILSE: But it's not enough. The main thing we wanted to identify with our Ikea collection [which was designed in 2015] wasn't just the notion of an object's function but instead the material qualities that create magic. The feeling of things—the magic of things—is really important. Beauty is one of those words that's been off the agenda for a long time, and people are uncomfortable talking about it.

> "Your experience of being in a space is often defined by the six inches around you much more than the space you can see beyond that."

HUGO: Beauty is aesthetic with feeling attached to it, basically—it not only looks good, but it touches you. It goes one step beyond aesthetics.

ILSE: Exactly—it transports you in some way. It's not an agreed code: It brings in the unmeasurables. We want more magic in the public sphere too, as the public space has been rationalized out of existence in many cases.

What service does public versus private space provide? Or are they morphing into one space too? Avi Friedman used the example of how cafés in the city are beginning to look more like our lounge rooms as our homes get smaller and we need to seek that kind of space elsewhere.

ILSE: In the 18th century, the coffee shop was the place where politics and life were hammered out—so many ideas were born there! In our work, we frequently talk about this idea of being at home in public space. We're reclaiming the space for ourselves instead of it belonging to others: It's our space.

It now goes beyond private and public space and into the third dimension of social media—Avi mentioned how it has become the "public square" of today. We used to interact with each other on the streets, but now we're seeking a lot of that social interaction online. How is that changing our spaces?

HUGO: The new third place is virtual. This means that physical public spaces have to be more compelling than they once were to hold our attention away from our smartphones and social media. It's depressing to see four people around a table in a restaurant all buried in their phones, but it's a common sight.

ILSE: It's not enough to say that you can get a lot of people into a space—you actually have to create spaces where people *want* to be and spend time with each other.

HUGO: The experience is really the principle thing: I'd say we've moved forward from an age of objects to an age of experiences.

Houses in the suburbs are getting bigger while apartments in cities are becoming more compressed—why do you think we're experiencing a simultaneous shrinking and expanding of our homes?

HUGO: People who live in the center of cities in tiny apartments know they have to trade space for the convenience of living in the city, whereas people in the suburbs accept they'll have a longer commute in order to have bigger homes and more space.

ILSE: And in the city, you don't necessarily need to use your home as a social space. But in the suburbs, you *need* it to be your social space.

In terms of trade-offs for those living in smaller apartments in the city, how do you think our homes can best adapt to our new situations? Or should we be the ones adapting to our new smaller homes?

HUGO: We talk about elastic space and fluid space, which are different ways of saying that space is at such a premium in our homes now. Whether the chicken comes before the egg—and it's actually our lives that are becoming more fluid just to accommodate the smaller spaces—I'm not sure.

ILSE: Homes must reflect changing living patterns. Based on the studies we've done, I think the kitchen is a very important spot—it might have different expressions and manifest itself in different ways because, culturally, we all cook differently—but that doesn't stop the fact that it's the hub. It's the evolution of the fire in the cave, the hearth: There needs to be that anchor in a home, but the size of it should be fluid depending on your space and needs. As for the rest of the home, it has to be responsive to the user's habits—it must be open enough to be a manifestation of people's actual behavior. You can't be too prescriptive about the size of these spaces nowadays because you don't know what shape the family will be or what their preferences are. It's about making spaces that people can adapt and adopt themselves.

PHOTOGRAPHS
PELLE CRÉPIN

STYLING
RUTH HIGGINBOTHAM

CASTING
SARAH BUNTER

Compare and Contrast

Crimson with burgundy, indigo with cobalt, mustard with cornflower, cerulean with turquoise: Unless you've equipped your life with Pantone swatches, you'll never find a perfect palette match, but that doesn't mean you can't enjoy the evocative power of color's hue-and-fro.

SWEATER BY PROENZA SCHOULER AT NET-A-PORTER*; TURTLENECK BY UNIQLO *PLEASE SEE CREDITS ON PAGE 158 FOR DETAILS

KINFOLK

SWEATER BY PROENZA SCHOULER AT NET-A-PORTER

SWEATER BY JIL SANDER

SHIRT AND SWEATER* BY Z ZEGNA

DRESS BY ACNE STUDIOS*

SWEATER BY JOSEPH

SWEATER AND TROUSERS BY PAUL SMITH

SHIRT BY Z ZEGNA; SKIRT BY JOSEPH

INTERVIEW
MARY STUTZMAN

PHOTOGRAPHS
ANDERS SCHØNNEMANN

A Day in the Life: New Tendency

Manuel Goller and Sebastian Schönheit believe in constantly redefining the norm and crafting fresh modes of thinking—which is why they decided to name their design studio New Tendency. We spoke to the co-founders of the Berlin-based practice about the importance of collaboration when designing timeless objects.

Some designers take their homework very seriously. Manuel Goller and Sebastian Schönheit met while studying at the Bauhaus University in Weimar, Germany, where they shared school projects and a passion for making contemporary furniture designed to suit the needs of a digital society. The town's small population, along with the school's interdisciplinary approach and its famed history, led to the pair starting self-initiated projects with graphic designers, product designers and artists. Since forming New Tendency in 2012, they've expanded their repertoire of objects to include everything from shape-shifting bookshelves to clean-line coat racks. They explain how a designer's work and home will never be truly finished.

What were your initial impressions of each other, and how have those impressions changed over time? — *Manuel (right):* Our friend [photographer Ina Niehoff] introduced us to each other—she invited us to drink red wine in front of the Henry van de Velde building in Weimar on a nice late summer day. I met Sebastian and could tell he was a calm and thoughtful person, and always up for a joke.
Sebastian (left): Manuel was high-flying, enthusiastic and always open-minded, but with a strong vision. Even though it took a few years until we started working together on a regular basis, we started to develop ideas immediately.

How does the concept of community play into your designs? — *Manuel:* We work as a team on all of our designs—creative dialogue is very important to us. We're lucky to have a broad network of friends and creative colleagues here in Berlin that we exchange ideas with constantly. That said, we make pretty quick decisions in the final design process, which are certainly influenced by others' opinions but are mostly intuitive.

What do each of you bring to the creative process? — *Manuel:* The creative process comes pretty naturally. We generally share the same sense of design, and after years of collaboration, we often just have to bring up a reference or keyword to both imagine the same picture. Of course, sometimes we also have opposite views on a certain design issue, but we use our collective energy to make the final product a better one.

Sebastian: Manuel and I are not the only ones involved in the product development—the whole team and our assistants play a big part in the process too.

Manuel: Shortly after I founded the studio, it became a three-man operation when Sebastian and I started collaborating, and my brother Christoph joined too—he's responsible for all the business operations and enables us to focus on the creative work. Now we're a seven-person team. In the first years, we enjoyed working by ourselves: We like the direct approach within a small team; that's also a reason why we don't want to grow too quickly. But on the other hand, we really like the dialogue and dynamic within a growing team. It's just beautiful when our co-workers can identify with our work like we do.

How do you make people see "everyday objects" in different ways? Why is this important to your work? — *Manuel:* Our design approach is quite conceptual in the beginning: We invest in a lot of thought and conversation before we even make the first stroke. When we start doing sketches or paper models, we shape the idea first—like a sculptor—by removing pieces of an imaginary prototype. During that process we carve out the object's character, which makes the difference.

Sebastian: Yes, we believe that each of our products has its own unique character. We also differentiate from others in terms of production—all our products are handmade in Germany. We're kind of obsessed with the quality of our products, and that's why we choose suppliers that we can visit and talk to in person.

How do you consider the user's needs when designing new objects? — *Manuel:* Our work is based on the topology of everyday objects. The user's need becomes the essence of our creations. Today that sometimes gets equated with technical, functional requirements only—we like to go beyond that and explore the audience's intellectual, poetic and cognitive demands.

What traditional design rules do you believe in, and which do you believe should be broken? — *Manuel:* We think it's very important to be aware of all traditional design rules: If you know the rules, you feel safer breaking them. It's kind of like playing the piano—if you know the keyboard and notes well, it's way easier to start improvising.

Are you both endless perfectionists? — *Sebastian:* Yes, we are! And endless is the point here—when it comes to our own designs, the work process never comes to an end. There's always something we want to improve, even if it's just a subtle perception.

Left: Sebastian and Manuel visit galleries and museums to glean inspiration from Berlin's modern architecture. Here they explore Galerie Johann König, a former church designed in the Brutalist style.
Above: The team always takes lunch together, either eating in the studio or heading to a nearby restaurant, such as Nathanja & Heinrich.

How have you learned to compromise by working with other people's creative visions? — *Sebastian:* The designers we've collaborated with are good friends. For us, it's not a compromise to work with other people: It's a challenge and an opportunity to create a unique product. We work eye-to-eye with them, so it feels more like a fun, creative game of Ping-Pong rather than making compromises.

Do you try not to be too influenced by others' work, or do you think that sharing ideas is important for creativity? — *Manuel:* To be honest, we don't look up the work of our contemporaries very often—not because we don't like to, but because we're simply trapped in our own little world too much. What really inspires us is contemporary art and architecture, and Berlin is a good place to enjoy both. This city is full of variety and change, so I think the best way to summarize the scene is to describe its diversity.

What consistent work routines do you keep? — *Manuel:* Since all our suppliers work really early in the morning, we usually start the day quite early. The first thing we do when we get to the studio is a status meeting where we update each other on all the things going on that day. We usually have a lot of phone calls and meetings about ongoing projects and products, but we cook or go out for lunch together every day. It's nice to have a break from work after

the first segment of the day. We enjoy having lunch together and exchanging ideas or projects we're currently working on—or just talking about food and new recipes!

Where do you live? How has your apartment been designed and how has that influenced your home life? — *Sebastian:* I live in a typically Berlin Altbau building with big rooms and windows. It's near the Spree River and not far from a park—that's what I like. I share the apartment with an old friend, Flo, who I also met at the Bauhaus University. Flo is a DJ, so in the evenings we spend a lot of time listening to music and talking about our projects. I have a collection of items I really like to have around me: a few books, my favorite pair of shoes and a pendant lamp by Konstantin Grcic. For me, those objects make me feel at home, even if I move to a new place.

Manuel: I live in a building in the Mitte neighborhood that was designed by Hans Poelzig in the Neue Sachlichkeit style: It's a compact flat compared to the stereotypical super-high-ceiling Berlin Altbau homes. I like the charm of it though; the interior is rather subtle. Now that it's getting to be winter again, I really enjoy reading at home or inviting friends over to hang out. My apartment is filled with prototypes or collector's items made by my friends. I like the idea of my flat being a test environment—a place that always makes me think of new products. In that sense, it should never be complete.

Left: Located in Berlin's Neukölln neighborhood, New Tendency's storefront features some of their latest products including the X-chair (left) and the META side table (right). Manuel stumbled upon the former electrical supply store on his walk home after apartment hunting and immediately fell in love with the postwar architecture.

WORDS
DIANA BUDDS

PHOTOGRAPHS
JUSTIN FANTL

Connecting the Lots

City planners may shape streets and devise green spaces,
but building community really starts where the pavement ends.
Participatory design is a diplomatically driven method
of development that listens to both stakeholders and local voices
to create a neighborhood where stories and streetscapes are shared.

Gazing at a city from 1,000 feet above the ground reveals a fascinating—and complex—narrative of modern-day urbanism. Based on the shape of streets, the layout of houses, their density and the dominant colors, a city's character comes into focus—as do the lives of the people who live there.

Take these aerial photographs of Phoenix, Arizona, as an example. Ambitious residential developments such as Arrowhead Lakes in the Glendale neighborhood are built around a sea of blue water. Lush green lawns lay adjacent to arid desert. Highway off-ramps lead to nowhere and paved street grids eagerly await neighborhoods to sprout up around them. While the lined-up houses each have their own postage stamp yards, there's not a park to be seen, nor a café or corner pub. These omissions reflect the actions of planners and developers who build cities based on speculation, not people. While the signs of civilization are there, the citizens

themselves are noticeably absent, and this lack of interaction diminishes the sense of community. And this is all by design.

The United States had a major growth spurt in the 20th century when policymakers and developers formed cities with industry and efficiency at the heart of decision making: It was about expanding the highway system, getting cars from point A to B, building parking spaces for those vehicles and designing sprawling intersections for them to safely cross paths. Architects proposed "visionary" projects that, on paper, would improve urban life. However, the polar opposite occurred as they based their objectives on assumptions of what people required, not what communities desired.

As we consider what makes a place desirable, it boils down to championing people. The good news is that decades of top-down planning have given way to bottom-up innovation as the community is now welcomed at the table. Much of this formal community

81

involvement is called *participatory design*, an umbrella term for workshops, activities, surveys, visioning sessions and interviews that call upon experiences and input from all stakeholders in a project—including the government, neighborhood members, developers and designers—not just the traditional decision makers at the top. The hope was that involving the community affected by a project would yield a stronger design.

Also called cooperative design or co-design, the participatory concept originated in Scandinavia and made its way to the United States in the 1960s. During this decade, pioneering activists like the great Jane Jacobs issued a rallying cry for planners to listen to people, take the pulse of a successful neighborhood and try to reverse engineer it for new initiatives instead of imposing prede-termined master plans. In fact, it's thanks to Jacobs that New York

City did not demolish parts of the West Village and SoHo, two of the city's most iconic enclaves, in favor of an expressway: While it would have supposedly improved traffic flow from Brooklyn to the Holland Tunnel, construction of the four-lane freeway would have razed Washington Square Park, which is a beloved public space and the heart of the community to this day. Her neighborhood-saving endeavors illustrate the root of the issue: As cities hold the purse strings for capital projects, rezoning and permitting development, bad design fundamentally boils down to bad policy.

"Many of our policies are built out of fear," says Jason Rob-erts, co-founder of The Better Block. His organization leads grassroots exercises on ways the community can improve their neighborhoods and also consults with local governments on how to incorporate citizen-led design into the bureaucratic process.

"Rules are typically put in place because of the fear that something horrendous could happen—which could be valid, I don't want to minimize that—but once you start constructing your community based on fear, your byproduct will be these structures that are inhumane," Roberts says. A classic example of this notion of "hostile" or "defensive" architecture is park benches that people can't lie on: Spacing the seats a certain way is a subtle modification intended to prevent homeless people from sleeping on them, but it also restricts how the seats are used by the rest of the population. "Your options are fear or love," he says. "When you look at an environment built on love, you get an entirely different ethos: You get an area with a high quality of life that shines and is very human-centered."

The Better Block started in 2010 when Roberts gathered a few friends together to stage a pop-up intervention in a section of Oak Cliff, a rougher neighborhood in Dallas, Texas. They banded together and spent an afternoon painting bike lanes, bringing in potted plants and trees, propping up a few café chairs and creating mock-ups of businesses in the empty storefronts. Once they were set up, they used the neighborhood like it was just another vibrant street. The hope was that by showing how easy it was to create a welcoming space in an area that was previously abandoned— thereby altering the psychology of the block—the city would take note and change some of its policies.

While the project was ephemeral (Roberts likens it to an art project), its effects weren't. Their act of building an attractive and vibrant city block sparked community. Since then, his team has replicated this process of faux-placemaking across the country. "Time and time again, I see people come out to these projects and say,

'I just want to work with my hands and do something,'" Roberts says. "Humans are made to move and made to be social. When people do some kind of physical activity together, it benefits the broader community and brings a sense of engagement."

On a larger scale, New York City is in the process of redesigning Flushing Meadows Corona Park—897 acres of open space in the borough of Queens. Originally built for the 1939-1940 World's Fair, seven million people now annually visit the park despite the fact that it hasn't been seriously updated for the past 50 years. To find out how to best bring the park into the 21st century, the Design Trust for Public Space, a non-profit advocacy group, has been engaging in participatory design initiatives with the surrounding communities. Sam Holleran, a participatory design fellow at Design Trust, has been working on visual materials to aid the process and has designed the curriculum for community learning sessions. He thinks that participatory design, when implemented at the right time and in a meaningful way, unites people and builds better results for the end users. "Involving community is not just about taking an approach that brings in equity and social justice," he says. "It's about making spaces that are durable. There's less objection to the design and less revision."

Some of the more apparent benefits of participatory design can be seen in master-planned neighborhoods. A 2008 study from California Polytechnic State University researcher Esther Valle showed that residents living in places that were built using participatory design methods felt a stronger sense of community and a deeper connection with their neighborhood. The residents of Bernal Gateway Apartments in San Francisco and Oak Court Apartments

in Palo Alto, two enclaves built using participatory methods, were interviewed about their satisfaction with their living environments. The study found that they use their neighborhoods' communal meeting spaces for socializing and feel more comfortable asking their neighbors for a favor, such as borrowing a cup of sugar, than residents of New Urbanist neighborhoods, which are built using another contemporary design method that promotes walkable environments but without participatory design efforts. The study concluded that while it's difficult to unequivocally say that either method alone is a primary contributor to creating community, involvement with the design creates attachment to a place, which in turn brings a stronger sense of community. Because people are encouraged to work together during the planning process, it sows the seed for interaction afterward.

Participatory budgeting is another strategy that builds community. This concept sets aside part of a civic budget and allows citizens to vote by committee on how to use it. In open forums, local leaders and their constituents meet, propose projects and decide what should get funded. "Participatory budgeting processes always focus on in-person meetings that bring people into rooms with their neighbors," says Josh Lerner, executive director of the Participatory Budgeting Project, a nonprofit that empowers people to collectively decide how to spend public money. "By creating new conversations, the community comes together around shared needs. The best way to understand what a community needs is to ask them, and the best way to meet those needs is to give the community real power to make the solutions happen through direct control over a budget."

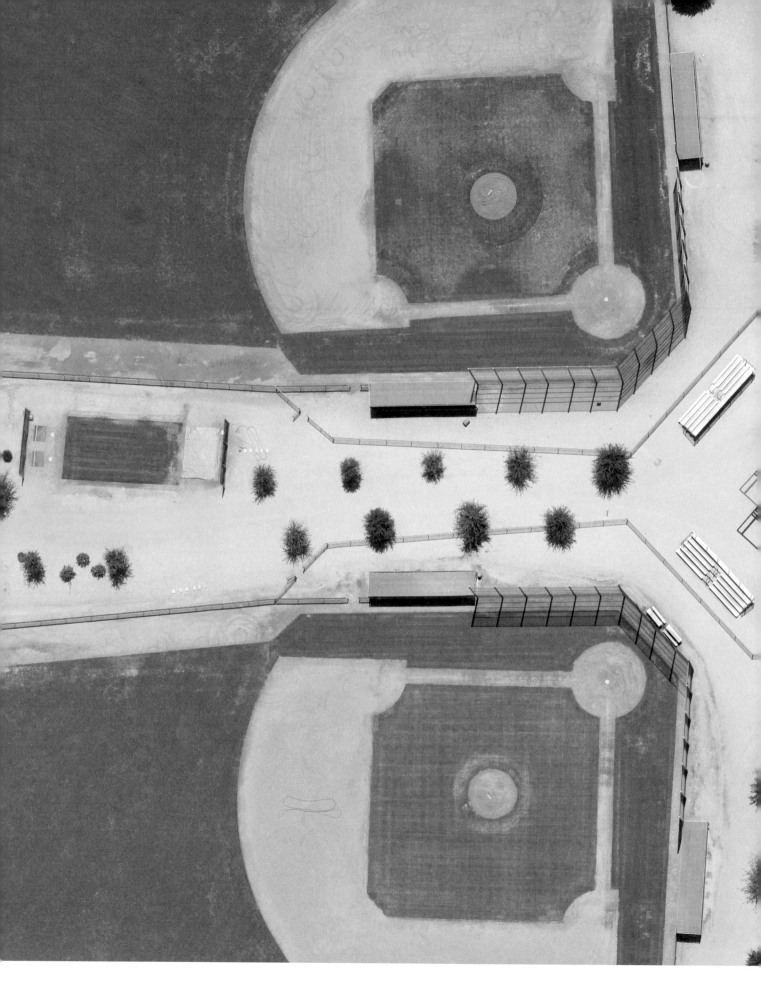

In Vallejo, California, a $3.2 million participatory budgeting allotment rallied 4,000 people around community gardens, new streetlights, road repairs, park improvements and senior citizen programs, among others. Prior to the process, city council members thought the residents wanted more police and public safety. But after engaging with the community, they found that while safety was a concern, it wasn't the only thing. People voiced their desire for parks, saw what needed to be done to get them and took action. "Some of the gardens have turned blighted, unused lots into vibrant gathering spaces in residential neighborhoods, while other green spaces have paved the way for new education and training programs in public schools and churches," says Ginny Browne, West Coast Project Manager at the Participatory Budgeting Project. The new gardens provide a much-needed "third place" for residents to

enjoy and nurture. With home referred to as the "first place" and work as the "second place," third places are important social areas for spontaneous interactions, such as coffee shops, bars and parks.

In addition to jump-starting civic projects, participatory budgeting also builds stronger trust between the city and citizens. "It was a time when Vallejo's residents' trust in city government was at an all-time low, and residents themselves were deeply divided over the reasons for the municipal failure," Browne says. "Through participatory budgeting, residents were able to sit across the table from city staff to talk through project ideas, learn about costs and feasibility and share their own knowledge about what was and wasn't working in their communities. We saw learning on both sides of the table, and both residents and city staff came away with a new sense of the value of collaboration." Coming together made the

planning process transparent to the community, taught them how to get their voices heard and helped them arrive at a shared vision for what their neighborhoods could become.

In his work with The Better Block, Roberts travels the world to share what he has discovered through speaking with people about their worries concerning a diminishing sense of neighborhood kinship and togetherness. What he's learned is that because of the fast pace of modern living and the detachment from communal social structures, people have slowly drifted apart from each other and are searching for ways to find their way back by working together in their neighborhoods. "There's an overall sense that we're not engaged as a community," Roberts says. "There's a void, and that void comes back to the fact that we used to do things together, craft our places together and look after each other, and we're not

doing that anymore. People feel like they're missing their tribe because of this."

Perhaps the way to reverse the years of disbanding is to take an active role in building and designing communities that reflect our shared desires, whether it's a park, streetscape or neighborhood that promotes a connected, slower life. Think of the difference between knitting a scarf versus buying one in a shop: the former is a point of pride you'll take care of to ensure it'll last a lifetime, whereas the latter will never earn the same regard. We should be living in neighborhoods we're proud of contributing to and reflect who we are. We should want to cherish them and pass them down to the next generation like a well-loved heirloom. The way to maintain that legacy—or to even build one from scratch—is not through having one voice heard; it's through a chorus of community involvement.

WORDS
SARAH OWEN

PHOTOGRAPHS
MATTHEW SPROUT

It's the coalescence of life's little details that creates the most fulfilling whole. From relishing in the comfort of humdrum routines to scouring the shoreline for flotsam, Michele Oka Doner weaves the human-made and natural elements of her day to find balance in both. The acclaimed artist reflects on what she's learned about the importance of interdependence, emotional intelligence and finding macro meaning in the world around her.

Natural Perspective
Michele Oka Doner

Michele Oka Doner

Michele Oka Doner

Miami-born, New York-based artist Michele Oka Doner has just celebrated her 70th birthday. With an impressive oeuvre of sculptures spanning more than five decades, Michele has developed the ability to simultaneously look both inward and outward—to notice the details in the everyday and then be able to place them in the context of the world at large. Though she has written books, designed objects and crafted furniture, she is most known for transforming organic materials into sculptures that intertwine animal, botanical and human forms. It's through this fusion of concepts that she's come to understand the significant connection between human-made and natural environments.

A childhood spent collecting fragments on Miami's beaches led Michele to a to a life transfixed by nature. Her surroundings were soaked in the chaotic elements that Florida is notorious for— think sudden and short-lived tropical storms quickly followed by exotic birds frolicking in newly formed puddles. "The tropics were fast and furious—like the dancing—and I was very aware of it as a power and a force," she says. "I remember the smell and the sight of the Everglades burning in the late '40s; I've always been aware of the cycles of nature—not in a soft way, but in a very ferocious way."

Born in a pre-television era, Michele spent her formative years playing outdoors with her neighboring epiphytic friend, the banyan tree. Through her time swinging on its branches, her environmental awareness of the surrounding soil and roots was piqued, and this mindfulness was paired with an inquisitive disposition bestowed to her by her father. "He would pause to watch the horizon," she says. "He didn't love flowers—it was the grander nature. The bigger picture. The scope as opposed to the particular." Michele adopted this macro outlook to her own world, seeking solace in nature's refuge as a place to escape America's artificial facade, which exploded in her early teens when the television hit en masse. "That wasn't the life that I found interesting—I found much more interest in the nature around me," she says. "It provided a sanctuary for me, as well as a place to *unself*—to come out of myself."

As part of this process of *unselfing*, Michele began to use art as an outlet to explore the different facets of her personality. She initially used metal as her main medium before experimenting with an array of materials, eventually delving into designing jewelry, furniture and freestanding sculptures. Made out of organic materials such as clay, cast bronze, porcelain and wax, her life-size figures mimic the truncated, quasi-ruined state of fossilized artifacts while also containing expressionistic, elemental qualities such as branches for arteries and roots for veins.

Her masterpiece to date, *A Walk on the Beach*, is one of the largest public art installations in the world. Initially completed in 1995 and extended in 1999, the mile-long concourse is housed in Miami International Airport and inlaid with almost 9,000 bronze effigies and mother-of-pearl fragments embedded in terrazzo. Walking along the giant sculpture feels like transcending into a cosmic version of the bottom of the ocean—a suitable voyage for visitors coming and going from Miami's surreal marine playground.

"I rarely look over my shoulder. You lose energy when you look back, and you can't see who's following you either. You have to look ahead and just keep going."

Michele Oka Doner

Creating art that temporarily transports the viewer into an otherworldly mindset is integral to Michele's practice. *Radiant Site*, another of her large-scale public pieces, features 11,000 tiles that resemble a larger-than-life wall of gold-foiled bricks in New York's Herald Square subway station. Intended to induce a "moment of respite" in the commuters' daily grind, the metallic tunnel creates an inverted void where you descend into light instead of darkness. Michele's inspiration for the piece was drawn from "all the places in the world where there's been something that stopped me and made me consider another realm, another self," she says. "I wanted to bring that feeling to somebody who's on automatic—just coming and going on a busy day."

This was the kind of reminder that Michele sought when she first moved away from Miami's natural wonderland. After receiving a Bachelor of Science in Design and her Masters of Fine Arts from the University of Michigan, she moved to Manhattan in the early '80s. It was a gritty and derelict time when the city was hard and unapologetic, and though there was a stream of culture flowing through the streets, the promise of creativity was often overwhelmed by the city's hardships. But by tapping into her father's worldy appreciation of the broader strokes, Michele found a way to see a different kind of nature in the city's landscape: The patterns of cracks in the sidewalk "ran like leaves' veins" and strips of seaweed crushed by delivery trucks in Chinatown resembled an above-water seascape. Seeing New York through a botanist's lens opened Michele up to a different view of what constituted a natural environment. You don't need to catch the subway up to Central Park to feel closer to nature; you just have to redefine it.

"Nature is everywhere in New York," Michele says. "Look out the window here—this is a very natural environment. Some of it's man-made, but it's made out of raw materials: brick, clay, stone. SoHo is paved with a geologist's dream!" With slate and bluestone from the quarries in upstate New York and an enormous collection of cast-iron architecture, lower Manhattan boasts a wealth of nature. Between the Ginkgo trees and the granite, it's here that Michele now calls home. "I'm living in a 19th-century village—this is the largest historic district for cast-iron in the world," she says, gesturing to the Greek-inspired columns in the space where she both lives and works.

Sitting above SoHo's cobblestones, Michele's airy 4,800-square-foot loft (445 square meters) feels one part museum and one part laboratory—a physical embodiment of Michele's attraction

to dichotomies. The work she creates in this sun-drenched studio blurs the boundaries of human and nature and challenges the anthropocentric worldview. Scattered oddities and found objects collected from the cosmos have an ordered chaos about them. Snippets of coral, twigs, tree roots, dried palm leaves and mummified insects add texture to her possessions—which include crystal fishbowls and bronze candelabras—as well as objects she has crafted herself from raw materials, such as glazed terra-cotta toasting cups and bark-shaped sterling silver serving forks.

"Working with organic materials and making things invigorates and enlivens the ritual of everyday life," she says. "I'm not looking to make something that lasts forever—I want to work on things that seem to have been there forever and can seamlessly move into an undefined and undesignated future." Her job as a metalworker is ancient, and she credits her maker skills to a pre-industrial era where blacksmiths and potters would fashion goods within the village. "This time wasn't so far back in our DNA, so it wasn't hard for me to pick up strands of it," she says. "Everything people had, they knew where it came from—they knew who made it, and they knew their neighbors."

From the farmers for her food to the master printer for her artwork, Michele is acutely aware of humanity's interdependence. "Community is beyond important; it's a necessity for survival," she says. "To think you're independent is a fallacy to me. We evolved to be dependent on each other, and that's still true—that's what makes us human." In this way, Michele has built her own kindred community; she's self-aware enough to know when she's lacking a skill, and savvy enough to find someone who can help her. For example, her large-scale framed works in the studio involve numerous collaborators: She sources paper from Wildwood Press in St. Louis, tracks down wood for the frames from the Philippines and then has a small, local business in TriBeCa put it all together.

One of the ways Michele has forged connections between ideas and people is through drawing from the wealth of knowledge in her enviable personal library. Reading has allowed her to escape into others' lives and has acted as a catalyst for her own curiosity. She sporadically peppers metaphors into conversations with such accuracy and eloquence that it's as if she was reading straight from a book's page. She has recently been poring over Shakespeare's *A Midsummer Night's Dream* in preparation for designing the sets and costumes for a new interpretation of George Balanchine's classic ballet choreography: The production, which celebrates Miami City Ballet's 30th season, has been reimagined in an underwater setting. Michele's designs use her Florida childhood as a muse and underscore Miami's intrinsic relationship with the ocean. This will be her first foray into costume and set design, but it isn't unusual for Michele to encounter challenges that extend beyond her past experiences. She's not afraid of undertaking projects that veer away from her comfort zone; in fact, she invites them.

Having enjoyed an amorphous career that has swung from printmaking to authorship, Michele's trajectory has always been

---

Previous spread: Items from Michele's past line her walls. They include photographs from her childhood growing up on the beaches of Miami, Florida, and an assortment of trinkets that she has collected over the years. Left: Michele combs through branches and pieces of driftwood in her SoHo studio. The large-scale black-and-white drawing in the background is a magnification of *nacre* (mother-of-pearl)—most of her sketches start with natural patterns like this. "I'm interested in forms," she says, "Whether it's from a seed or a tree, everything alive has to have veins to distribute the fluids of life. It's timeless."

99

diverse and self-initiated. Back when she was studying art in the '60s, the word *career* didn't exist in the art world, so students had to seek their own routes. "Since there was no pathway, it was a wonderful time to explore what our own meaning was. To find meaning for ourselves—that was the dialogue," she says. With no parameters, prerequisites or even expectations for professional longevity, the freedom of an undefined creative life was empowering.

Deciding to eschew the word *career*, she instead referred to her life and work as a *craft*—not the term riddled with associations of folksy knickknacks or unrefined designs, but instead as an artisanal approach to curating her thoughts and surroundings. "I've always liked the application of the word *craft*, as in *I've crafted a life*," Michele says. "You could craft your beer or you could craft your dinner: It's about selecting your best ingredients, putting them together and combining them to make something that's nourishing for you." By electing the elements that define her day-to-day—no matter how large or small those decisions may be—Michele lives a ceremonious life where rituals are revered, not glossed over. "When I set out to have my own home, my notion was to have something ceremonial that I would enjoy every day," she says.

Michele starts each morning by reaching for a "wonderfully large cup of coffee" before breakfasting on fresh fruit and yogurt. By the time she's at her desk around 8:30 a.m., she's already appreciated what some people might consider the mundane moments in their days. "You have teeth, but if you want to keep them and maintain them, you need to take care of them," she says. "Everything's a daily practice. There's no slacking off in life." This mantra—that we must be mindful and put effort into even the smallest of tasks— helps Michele sustain a routine where her attentiveness allows her to slow down and savor overlooked occasions.

While Michele's overarching quest is for orderly days, she's viscerally aware of the other end of the spectrum. "When you're willing to participate, to extend yourself, to go out of your comfort zone, to have a routine but break that routine, to listen and to be spontaneous, then you open yourself up to experience and to community," she says. A creature of habit, she's also completely comfortable—even encouraging—of unexpected moments being thrown into the fray. This contrast brings color to her life, even if that means turning unlucky incidents like getting a flat tire on the New Jersey Turnpike into a chance for adventure.

Michele's paradoxical love of both her spontaneous and more disciplined sides allows her to embrace moments for self-improvement. This has opened her up to all sorts of life lessons, such as acknowledging that being physically present doesn't necessarily mean that you're really there. She learned this when attending events despite not being in the mood. "If I'm very tired, I've learned not to go, because it'll go right by me—and that's frustrating," she says. "I don't ever want to be a passive participant. If I go, I want to engage." In a modern world where the fear of missing out is made all the more pervasive through the mirror of social media, being in control of our choice-making can make us feel empowered,

Michele Oka Doner

"Community is beyond important; it's a necessity for survival. To think you're independent is a fallacy. We evolved to be dependent on one another—it makes us human."

Michele Oka Doner

Michele Oka Doner

Michele Oka Doner

"When you're willing to participate, to go out of your comfort zone, to have a routine but break that routine, to listen and to be spontaneous, then you open yourself up to experience."

not just one of the herd. Choosing what we actually want to participate in helps us craft the best memories for the future, all the while enabling us to feel comfortable and involved in the present.

Applying discipline to our diaries is only the first step: Our mental health is as deserving of daily diligence. And that means acknowledging—and embracing—our idiosyncrasies. Drawing from her nature-based upbringing and nonconformist college years, Michele has come to disregard many traditional modes of judgment and instead believes in defining her own parameters. "We're learning that we're evolving and have more frequencies and intelligences than we realized," she says. Citing the original two intelligences—reading and math—Michele references the theory of eight distinct intelligences, which is a philosophy established by Harvard developmental psychologist Howard Gardner: intra-personal ("the ability to relate to other people"), interpersonal ("the ability to understand yourself"), visual-spatial, bodily-kinesthetic, musical, logical-mathematical, linguistic and naturalist.

The intelligences passed on to Michele weren't prescribed by textbooks. She even adds a ninth quality to Gardner's list: rural intelligence. She first recognized it in her grandfather, who grew up in the Russian woods. He used to whistle outside her window every morning to wake her for breakfast, and she came to learn the difference between his call and a swallow's. "I had a connection to somebody who knew what it was to be an agrarian. That was really wonderful," she says. Her mother's side of the family handed down a different skill set entirely. "My other grandfather came from scribes, and they were literate in a whole other way," she says. "I speak another language: not of the tongue, but of the eye."

The idea that intelligence is measured in many ways is freeing: It lifts the pressure to be brilliant at everything. Instead, we can concentrate on enjoyment for enjoyment's sake without feeling the need to succeed. "For example, I love to run, but I was never going to be a runner. I don't have the physical structure," Michele says. Her limitations haven't stopped her from indulging in the areas of life she loves, and understanding this division allows her to focus on fostering the areas where she excels. "It's a combination of physical attributes and what we're born with, and then we have to be willing to invest in those," she says. In the same way she's conscious of her time and energy, Michele constantly seeks betterment in all areas of her repertoire—even the parts that come naturally.

When she was a girl scouring the beach for jetsam, Michele noticed that everything she collected was a fragment: partial and imperfect. As a result, she's never been drawn to whole objects. A finished product does not equal fulfillment, because once it's complete, what is there left to learn or improve on? Michele takes the same attitude in her own life. "I'm on a path and I'm looking forward. I rarely look over my shoulder. You lose energy when you look back, and you can't see who's following you either," she says. "You have to look ahead and just keep going."

The challenge from age 70 to 80? To forge ahead as if it were just the beginning.

Left: When Michele moved to New York City in 1981, she brought an appreciation of organic elements with her. She believes that we can find nature in even the most constructed places if we look close enough. "This is a very natural environment: There are Ginkgo trees that turn gold and dozens of different stones within just a few blocks from here," she says, motioning down the steet in SoHo. "I know where to walk at different times of the year. You can see the marks of how the stones were extracted from the earth and how the rain has hit them over the years—the city is speaking all the time."

PHOTOGRAPHS
NEIL BEDFORD

STYLING
CAMILLA POLE

CASTING
SARAH BUNTER

Order in the Courts

Sporting endeavors keep us in shape and form shapes of their own: From baseball's diamonds and snooker's triangles to the goal lines we protect and the running tracks we circle, we take a closer look at the graphic patterns inherent in the athletic field.

FOR CLOTHING CREDITS,
PLEASE TURN TO PAGE 158

WORDS
JORDAN KUSHINS

EMPATHETIC DESIGN

When our fundamental needs, desires and abilities are considered before the creative process begins, the end result offers a balance between simple beauty and just-so function. Similar to the emotional support we give to our loved ones, human-centered design can provide comfort as well as service.

Knowing thyself can be tough, but knowing others—really, truly *feeling* them—is a true skill. Empathy is one of the fundamental ways we understand and relate to each other, giving us the capacity to sense and share the emotions of those around us: the way your heart hurts when a friend goes through a breakup; the exhilaration when an underdog bests the reigning champ; the apprehension of watching someone prepare to make an important speech. These sentimental moments are the lifeblood of emotional intelligence.

Empathy starts in the heart but eventually hooks up with the mind. It's innate, but it can be learned. Which means it can be taught. Which, of course, means it can be designed.

Design is ubiquitous. Products and architecture, hardware and software, programs and services—all of these things have been, on some level or another, designed. Perhaps that's why the concept of empathetic, human-centered design can be a bit of a mind-bender: If empathy is the very intimate ability to understand your fellow compatriots on a sensitive and experiential level, how can something inanimate be imbued with that same kind of emotional depth?

Empathetic design is as much about the creative process as it is the final product. Designers who practice this methodology first look deeply at who they're designing for: What are their needs? What are their capacities? What do they really desire? At this stage of the process, research is more social than strictly academic; it's about tapping into those essential factors on a personal level through careful observation and sensitive questioning. This line of soft interrogation helps designers suss out the underlying problems, and then they come up with a solution that's best suited for the user. Roman Krznaric, the philosopher, writer and author of *Empathy: Why*

> "Empathy starts in the heart but hooks up with the mind. It's innate, but it can be learned. Which means it can be taught. Which, of course, means it can be designed."

It Matters, and How to Get It, calls this process "outrospection."

In this way, the act of creation can be exceptionally democratic: of people, by people, for people. Its reach can range from niche market to mass consumption and has the potential to impact us on every level from life-brightening (a soft-white Cree LED bulb engineered to glow warmly instead of with a standard blue tinge) to life-altering (a dedicated bike lane installed on your daily route to and from the office). Small changes in design can make a massive difference, especially when coupled with a lesson that Spider-Man learned at an early age: With great power comes great responsibility.

The people-first mentality and our attitudes toward it have evolved dramatically since the 1960s, when early forms of the movement emerged under the umbrella of "universal design": This term was coined by Ronald L. Mace, an architect, industrial designer and educator who campaigned for a world that accommodated everyone regardless of their age, physical ability or cognitive aptitude.

That goal may seem obvious now, but at the time, it was a groundbreaking thought. Consider the street's curb as an everyday example of pre- and post-empathetic design. Around the world, many pedestrians navigate their way on sidewalks that flank the streets. These paths are slightly raised from the pavement for a number of reasons (primarily to guide wastewater to gutters and as a visual and tangible barrier between cars and citizens) and that slight step up or down is a simple one for many folks on foot. But for whole swathes of the population—including, but definitely not limited to, those with mobility impairment—it's often quite literally insurmountable.

In 1967, a British accessibility pioneer named Selwyn Goldsmith interviewed hundreds of wheelchair users in Norwich, England, as part of a civic case study for the second edition of his revolutionary book, *Designing for the Disabled*. The feedback was enlightening and inspired a straight-forward but surprisingly revolutionary *what-if?*: Instead of a sharp angle where the curb meets the road at crosswalks, could there be a gentle downgrade instead? An initiative was launched to turn that question into a concrete answer.

In a limited series of selected spots throughout the city, curbs were "cut" or "dropped." Most amblers might not have noticed this simple change, but it dramatically improved the ease with which other members of society could do something as simple as heading down the street to grab milk from the corner store. Goldsmith's experiment was taken up by numerous other countries, and this feature is now federally mandated by the Americans With Disabilities Act of 1990.

Taking the step to consider the practical needs of the user rarely weakens the aesthetic of a product—cutting the curb didn't diminish its design in the slightest, for example. On the contrary, considering all sorts of "functional limitations,"

"By abandoning preconceptions about what 'should' be made and focusing on what will benefit the user, empathetic designers see the solutions that are often hiding in plain sight."

as Valerie Fletcher, the executive director of the Institute for Human Centered Design, calls them, can actually enhance the way we interact with our environment and each other. "Design is a deeply rooted human practice—one that actually shapes the context of our lives," Fletcher says.

Gone are the stilted focus groups ushering a team of narrow-minded designers toward a client-approved, pre-determined goal. In their place, companies that let real-world observations of real people inform their decisions have begun to thrive.

IDEO has been honing this human-centered practice since they were founded in 1991. The Bay Area firm, which has since gone global, is now the archetype for the modern model of design thinking and has given a thoughtful new take on everything from school lunches to voting booths and Tempur-Pedic mattresses. "The best thing you have as a designer are your eyes and ears," says Paul Bennett, IDEO's Chief Creative Officer. "You drop your ego and go out into the world with an open mind." It's this heightened aptitude for impartial perception that can make human-centered design an unbiased—and unconventional—creative act.

Though the modern movement may still tout the "form follows function" mantra, form can only follow function once an object's true function has been determined. Rather than answering a concise client brief with an equally concise result, companies like IDEO make the "function" side of the equation their modus operandi from the get-go. This process requires an alchemical balance between sense and sensibility, between logic and the direct defiance of it. "I'd describe it as jazz," Bennett says. "We have the basic melody, but we improvise. Everything is about the chemistry between the people here and the people there. We observe, and the jazz takes over. The riffing is where we are very good."

If that all sounds quite free-form for a practical guide to coming up with smart, actionable solutions—it is. By abandoning preconceptions about what "should" be made or achieved and focusing on what will actually benefit the user, empathetic designers see the solutions that are often hiding in plain sight. "We have a phrase: A blinding glimpse of the bleeding obvious," Bennett says. In other words: People are complicated. As living, breathing, highly subjective and oh-so-complex beings, we are fallible by nature as both creators and consumers. We don't always know, or can't always clearly articulate, what we want: A good designer can anticipate the user's needs more effectively than the user can themselves. They make connections in surprising ways that clarify, simplify, then realize a way forward.

But then again, even the most well-conceived products can't be judged on the

"We don't always know, or can't always clearly articulate, what we want: A good designer can anticipate the user's needs more effectively than the user can themselves."

effectiveness of their functions alone—an object's aesthetic is vital to empathetic design in the same way our gut instincts inform our emotions in empathy's human form. In his 2004 book, *Emotional Design: Why We Love (Or Hate) Everyday Things*, cognitive scientist Don Norman proposes three levels to design. Before we weigh in on how well something works—our "behavioral" evaluation—we have an initial first impression. This is our like-it-or-not "visceral" take: an instinctual decision that happens in an instant as an immediate response to sensory factors such as sight and touch. It's superficial, sure, but significant.

Simply dismissing the importance of these first two levels of attraction denies the potent strength of pure, unadulterated aesthetic delight; that feeling when you see something—some *thing*—and become infatuated. Anyone who has ever swooned at the subtle curve of a soupspoon by David Mellor, *oohed* and *aahed* at the ever-so-slightly matte texture of a bud vase from Heath Ceramics or delighted at the soothingly geometric weave of a Turkish kilim rug knows it's possible to have affection for the inanimate world that's been built up around us.

Once our brains have weighed in on these first two verdicts, we balance out the "visceral" and "behavioral" aspects by getting to Norman's third level of design: "reflective." This is when we work out

something's overall significance to our lives: its message and its meaning, its image in the eyes of others and its usefulness and appeal to ourselves. It's both a tricky and highly subjective equilibrium. "No single product can hope to satisfy everyone," Norman says, but continuing to look at the world through an inclusive lens will pave the way—or rather, many complementary ways—for the next generation.

So what does the future look like? It's tactile maps and audio guides at transit stations, such as Bordeaux's pioneering Light Rail system. It's further acknowledging the plight of the delayed traveler by turning airports like San Francisco's Terminal Two into havens for local cuisine and comfortable lounging. It's the vegetable peelers and coffee makers and all those standard, day-to-day products that greatly affect our lives, from finding the perfect shower temperature in the morning to setting our alarms at night. It's designers the world over sharing narratives, regaling origin stories and giving insight into the fact that, as the late great IDEO co-founder Bill Moggridge once said, "There is nothing made by human beings that does not involve a design decision somewhere."

As the human experience continues to evolve, shifting as we grow and change as individuals and as a society, so too will the designers helping to guide the way down a path we all can travel together.

RECIPES
MIKKEL KARSTAD

PHOTOGRAPHS
ANDERS SCHØNNEMANN

STYLING
MIKKEL KARSTAD & SIDSEL RUDOLPH

The Black & White Menu

Despite being devoid of color, this menu is by no means short on taste—by limiting some of our senses, we can amplify others. Paired with some simple monochromatic serving suggestions, you can mix and match these delicious options to make a tabletop chessboard.

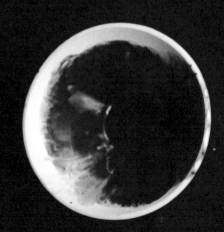

124

CELERIAC SOUP WITH PARSLEY ASH OIL

Seasoned with shavings of fresh celeriac and charred parsley oil, a bowl of this creamy broth will warm you all the way to your roots.

FOR THE CELERIAC SOUP

1 medium celeriac
2 tablespoons unsalted butter
1 shallot, sliced
2 ½ cups (600 milliliters) water
1 cup (240 milliliters) whole milk
Salt and freshly ground pepper
Parsley Ash Oil (recipe follows)

FOR THE PARSLEY ASH OIL

1 bunch flat-leaf parsley
¼ to ⅓ cup (60 to 75 milliliters)
    extra-virgin olive oil
Salt

CELERIAC SOUP

Trim the top and bottom from the celeriac and peel using a paring knife. Halve the root lengthwise. Using a mandoline, shave about 24 paper-thin, half-moon slices from one of the ends. Put the slices in a small bowl of cold water until the soup is served to keep their color bright. Coarsely chop the remaining celeriac.

Melt the butter in a medium pot over medium heat. Add the chopped celeriac and shallot and sauté until the shallot is translucent and the celeriac begins to soften, about 10 minutes.

Add the water and bring to a boil over medium-high heat. Reduce the heat and cook at a low simmer until the celeriac is tender, 5 to 7 minutes. Add the milk, season with salt and pepper and let the soup simmer for about 5 minutes more.

Blend the mixture in two batches until liquefied and completely smooth. Taste and adjust the seasoning as needed.

To serve, drain the celeriac slices. Pour the soup into warmed bowls, and arrange some of the sliced celeriac on top of each. Drizzle with the Parsley Ash Oil.

PARSLEY ASH OIL

Preheat the oven to 500°F (260°C). Trim the thick stems from the parsley bunch, just below the leaves, and discard. Spread the parsley on a large rimmed baking sheet and bake until completely black, dry and burned, about 10 minutes.

Put the parsley in a blender with ¼ cup oil and a big pinch of salt and blend until smooth, adding a little more oil if needed. Use immediately, or store in the refrigerator for several months.

SESAME-SEARED COD WITH FENNEL, DAIKON AND BLACK OLIVE VINAIGRETTE

Flaky fillets are doused in slightly sweet vinegar and finished with a peppery crunch to create a sharp combination of dark and light flavors.

⅓ cup plus 2 tablespoons (100 milliliters) extra-virgin olive oil

⅓ cup (75 milliliters) apple cider vinegar

1 teaspoon honey

Salt

¼ cup (40 grams) coarsely chopped black olives, such as cerignola or kalamata

10 whole black peppercorns

1 small fennel bulb, tops trimmed

4 ounces (115 grams) daikon radish, peeled

1 ½ pounds (680 grams) cod, cut into 4 to 6 fillets

Freshly ground pepper

About ½ cup (75 grams) black sesame seeds

To make the vinaigrette, whisk together ⅓ cup of the oil, vinegar, honey and 1 teaspoon salt. Stir in the olives. Crush the peppercorns with a mortar and pestle or the side of a large knife and add to the vinaigrette. Taste and adjust the seasoning as needed.

Thinly slice the fennel and radish using a mandoline. Put the vegetables in a bowl and cover with cold water while you prepare the fish to help keep their bright color and crispness.

Season the cod fillets generously with salt and pepper. Coat the fillets on each side with black sesame seeds, gently pressing them in to adhere.

Heat the remaining 2 tablespoons oil in a large sauté pan over medium heat. When the oil is hot, add the fillets and sear until the fish is just cooked through, turning once, about 3 minutes per side. Adjust the heat as needed to prevent the seeds from burning.

To serve, place each cod fillet on a plate. Drain the vegetables well and arrange them on top of the fish. Drizzle plenty of the vinaigrette over the fish and vegetables and serve.

VANILLA PANNA COTTA WITH PEAR, WHITE CHOCOLATE AND BLACK LICORICE

This softly set cream is served under a layer of paper-thin pears, dusted in licorice specks and sprinkled with white chocolate shavings.

2 teaspoons gelatin powder

2 tablespoons cold water

2 cups (480 milliliters) heavy cream

3 tablespoons sugar

½ vanilla bean pod

1 teaspoon white rum

1 stick black licorice

1 pear

White chocolate bar, for grating

Sprinkle the gelatin over the water in a medium heatproof bowl and set aside to soften, at least 5 minutes.

Put the cream and sugar in a small saucepan. Slice the halved vanilla bean pod lengthwise and scrape out the seeds. Add the seeds and pod to the pan with the cream mixture and bring to a simmer over medium heat, stirring occasionally. (Be careful not to let it boil over.)

Remove the pan from the heat and slowly pour the hot cream mixture into the bowl of softened gelatin, stirring to dissolve. Stir in the rum. Let the mixture cool for about 10 minutes, stirring occasionally. Discard the vanilla bean pod, cover the bowl and refrigerate until set, at least 4 hours.

To serve, freeze the licorice for 20 to 30 minutes to make it firm. Peel, quarter and core the pear, and slice it paper-thin using a mandoline. Arrange spoonfuls of the panna cotta on cold plates and place the pear slices delicately over the top. Dust generously with finely grated white chocolate and licorice.

WORDS
DANIELLE DEMETRIOU
GEORGIA FRANCES KING
SADIE STEIN
MARY STUTZMAN

PHOTOGRAPHS
PHIL DUNLOP
NICOLE FRANZEN
CHRISTIAN FRIIS
DAN GLASSER
NOEL MANALILI
ZOLTAN TOMBOR

Profile Series:
Design Committee

In one form or another, a good designer always has society's wishes at the opposite end of their pencil, paintbrush or stylus. Hailing from six countries, some of the designers in this feature are solo operators, others manage intercontinental teams and two are partners in both business and life. They design comfy couches, men's shirts, Moroccan hotels, non-profit logos and giant interactive ball pits: But most importantly, they design an experience that's shared by their community.

Alex Mustonen & Daniel Arsham, Snarkitecture

The founders of the interior installation firm talk about reshaping spaces into shared experiences that invite audiences to step outside the norm.

Blending their backgrounds in art and architecture, classmates Alex Mustonen and Daniel Arsham started Snarkitecture in 2008 and have been appropriating public spaces ever since. With projects ranging from "fun"iture to full-size social installations, they've made cement pillows for cell phones, carved caves into storefronts, created fabric tunnels out of 100,000 meters of white ribbon for fashion brand COS and even built a monochromatic ball pit beach using 750,000 clear recyclable balls inside Washington, D.C.'s National Building Museum. They spoke to us from Brooklyn about breaking down architectural boundaries, creating unexpected interactions and the importance of play for all ages.

How have your initial impressions of each other changed over time? — *Alex (right):* We met each other at Cooper Union in New York where I was studying architecture and Daniel was studying art. He was one of the few sculpture students that was sort of fascinated and obsessed with how architecture was put together.

Daniel (left): Alex had a very organized desk on the architecture floor and I had a very disorganized studio on the art floor. My impression was that he was extremely well organized and clean, and he's pretty much still like that.

How do your architecture-minded and art-minded brains balance each other out? — *Daniel:* I think I'm the "voice of dissent" in the studio and push ideas to places that they might not otherwise go. I often bring the team to a place that's challenging—the art background I have enables me to think about everything in that way.

Alex: Because I'm so interested in architecture and spend all my time thinking about it, I like to consider how things are put together and how to take the concepts we're developing in the studio and bring them into reality. I spend a lot of time thinking about how space and architecture affect our experiences of the everyday world. The character of architecture is incredibly important to me and shapes how I feel and look at my surroundings.

What are Snarkitecture's core values? — *Alex:* I think unexpectedness, reduction and simplicity are key. I love a good grid and a sense of order, but I also always enjoy pushing against that.

Daniel: And a kind of honesty and economy of materials so there's nothing superfluous.

Alex: In addition to these sorts of semi-serious things, the underlying, unspoken condition of our work is play—that there's a sort of subversion or invitation to engage with architecture and objects in a way that suggests playfulness.

Who comprises your personal and professional communities? — *Alex:* We often work collaboratively with people in other creative disciplines, such as fashion, art, design and music. That's our circle of colleagues and collaborators.

Daniel: We have friends who are artists and other architects, but I don't think our work is part of any specific group or movement—our community is the community we have in the studio. I think we surround ourselves with people who are very good at things

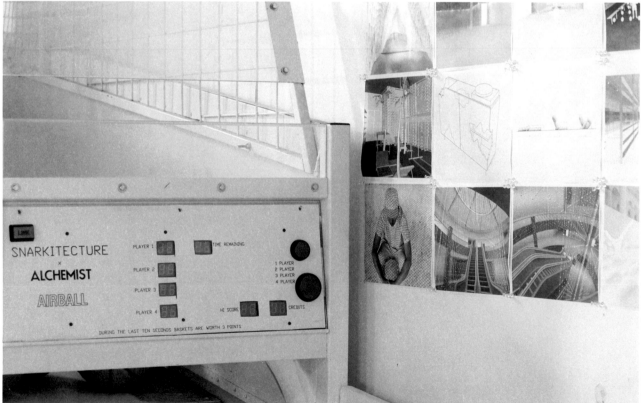

Above and opening spread: In addition to large-scale installations, Snarkitecture also designs "fun"iture and objects instilled with architectural humor. Founders Alex Mustonen and Daniel Arsham frequently use a monochromatic color scheme to allow the viewer to focus on a single element of their designs.

> "Unexpectedness, reduction and simplicity are key. I love a good grid and a sense of order, but I also always enjoy pushing against that."

that we don't know how to do, whether that's musicians or other designers.

Alex: The larger creative community we're connected to is not about style or content, but rather about the way they support, help and inform us—it's more of a friendship. I have a close group of people that I've been friends with for a very long time from childhood, school, Cooper Union and since then in New York. They're obviously part of my community, but I also think that my community is the studio: the group of people who are here every day working for Snarkitecture. We all support each other and we support each other's work.

What have you learned about the collective consciousness through orchestrating ideas in public spaces? — *Alex:* Part of that is the studio's collective consciousness: We operate in this collective environment that Daniel and I have started, but our growth has involved the collaboration of all the members of the team here.

Daniel: In terms of the creation of our work, we are often looking for things that people already know and recognize. We take existing spaces and try to manipulate and transform them. We tap into people's base knowledge of architecture and try to subvert that or invite people to think about it in a different way.

How do your installations break down boundaries? — *Daniel:* We often try to create scenarios that encourage people to engage with architecture as they did when they were children. The way that kids interact with and misuse architecture informs some of the types of things that we create.

Alex: We invite people to engage with architecture in a way that's outside of their regular day-to-day environment. So whether that's bringing the viewers back to a space that reminds them of their childhood or challenging them to actually physically engage with something, it creates a socially interactive space. We try to welcome people into this place of wonder where we break down the usual barriers. I think there's also something about collective environments and shared experiences— whenever you're having an experience that you're sharing with other people, it invites you to connect with them in a way that you wouldn't otherwise.

In terms of design, how have you seen technology change the concept of community in the past decade? — *Alex:* A lot of people see our work and then share it via social media, but even then, the initial experience is always rooted around physical interaction and physical engagement with objects and architecture. The 2015 version of experiencing these moments is to take a photo and post it somewhere, whereas 10 years ago you were actually telling people about it in person. But at the end of the day, it's still about making things, creating physical encounters and having visceral reactions instead of any sort of theoretical or visual world.

How important is it to consider the lifespans of the experiences you create? — *Daniel:* When we create something as Snarkitecture, we're looking to make something that's timeless. I don't mean that it's going to be relevant in 100 years— I mean that the work feels like it might've been made in different time periods. So it could've been made 10 years ago or 20 years ago, and in some cases the work has an even more historical feel to it.

Your designs are nearly always monochromatic. What does the absence of color bring to your work? — *Daniel:* In many cases, that absence of color is related to the re-forming of something that already exists. When we start a project, we don't think about adding anything to that space but rather transforming something that is already there. The big project we did for Design Miami in 2012 was a good example of that: They had this simple, vinyl event structure, and we took the vinyl material and created a new form out of it. It was a kind of alteration of the existing rather than an addition of something.

Alex: It's also about focusing and directing the visitor's experience toward either a simple concept or a single gesture, which brings them into an environment that's totally outside of normal life.

How do you know when a project is "done" and let yourself walk away from it? — *Alex:* The work is so experience-driven that we focus on what it's going to be like to be inside of it and how people will actually physically engage with it. So the "making of" the work is in some ways the least important part. When people are using it and it's continuing to evolve—that's when it's actually a piece of work. MS

Margaret Howell

By forgoing trends in favor of classic patterns with distinctive details, this London-based designer draws from her childhood memories to create simple pieces that defy eras.

Natural, unpretentious and definitively British: While sipping tea with designer Margaret Howell, it soon becomes clear that these adjectives can be applied to both the person as well as her designs. Few designers evoke a stronger sense of Britishness than Howell, who has quietly won a global following since launching her minimalist fashion label on her southeast London kitchen table in 1972. Today, there are six Margaret Howell stores in the UK, boutiques in Paris and Florence and more than 100 stores in Japan—her biggest market—including three cafés that serve English teas, cakes and a perfect winter shepherd's pie. Her understated clothing mixes modern tailoring with quality British heritage fabrics, and she also creates an equally popular line of household products and curates British design exhibitions at her London flagship store. One year shy of 70, Howell is modest and quietly spoken with an old-school charm—she doesn't even use email, so our pre-interview correspondence was suitably sent courtesy of Royal Mail. We asked her for advice about crafting timeless designs while staying focused purely in the moment.

How did your early years define your career path as a designer? — At school, I was always doing doodles of hairstyles, shoes, clothes and that sort of thing. Much later on, I found that some of the teachers' clothing came back to me when designing my collections. So I must have been sitting there looking like I was listening to the teacher, but I was really more interested in

her pinstripe suit: I suppose that, even then, I had an intuitive feel for a sense of current fashion. Meanwhile, I had a simple life with my parents. They would grow vegetables in the garden and serve them at picnics; we always self-catered and we'd go to places off the beaten track. That's what they liked, and that's what I love now. The style of my designs and the feeling of the clothes has a similar sort of naturalness; it's not a tight-fitted smartness. Fabric is key—as is authenticity—over something purely decorative or created for effect.

How do you imbue your personal value system into a physical product? — I try to give life and authenticity to my designs. It all starts when you have an idea about something—it could be triggered by an item of clothing or maybe a fabric. For me, it's often tied up with memory and association. For instance, the way I've designed my shirts has always been tied up with memories of my dad's old cotton shirts being worn-in, soft and crumpled.

What elements of design do we not realize affect our quality of life? — School design can have a big impact. Schools are functional buildings and should be well designed. I attended an experimental school in Burgh Heath, Surrey, and it was so brilliant and well built. It was a brick building with a large assembly hall and windows along one side, playing fields and a wonderful new gym. I remember on our first day people were still up on ladders doing little sculptural reliefs set into the bricks.

Right: Having designed her own clothing line since 1972, Margaret Howell's influences include actor Katharine Hepburn, pilot Amy Johnson and memories of her dad's crumpled shirts. She is pictured here wearing her SS15 dense cotton poplin PJ shirt and a pair of twill chinos made in collaboration with Edwin.

PHOTOGRAPH: PHIL DUNLOP

Unfortunately it was knocked down and the area was rebuilt during the Thatcher years, but it's interesting to think now about the influence it had on me.

How does the design of our homes influence our domestic lives? — A small house can appear to have a lot of space and light if it's well designed with the right proportions. It's incredible the effect a building has upon you without you realizing it—you don't have to be someone who appreciates aesthetics to be affected by it. And if you do appreciate aesthetics, it just fills you with more joy!

What is the difference between simplicity and minimalism? — In design, minimalism suggests the bare essentials. Editing out anything superfluous always makes it better; things become clearer. Minimalism

can be very sophisticated, of course, but simplicity suggests something more basic and charming. In terms of objects, if you look at a Lucie Rie pot, for instance, there is so much skill involved that you could hardly say it's simple, yet its shape and form are minimal in essence.

Your designs have long been regarded as quintessentially British. How important is "Britishness" as an ingredient in your creations? — I used to like the European magazines—the Italian and the French—as they were more in tune with my style. I liked their styling and take on English fashion. I actually didn't relate very much to the whole 1960s pop culture thing that went on here—all the minis and things. Where I looked to Britain was in terms of the people I used to make things, such as the fabric sources. British fabrics that've been made

here for a long time have a sort of depth to them. Rather than look at trends, I like to use real fabrics and then be innovative in the design or the type of clothing I'm making instead.

Whose design philosophies do you most respect? — The designers I was most influenced by in the 1960s and 1970s were Yves Saint Laurent and Jean Muir: There is a pared-down plainness to the make and quality of Jean Muir that I've always appreciated. As for Yves Saint Laurent, it was all about the tailoring and the trouser suit. I remember buying a Yves Saint Laurent pattern for a jacket when I was at art school—I learned a lot from it.

What else inspires your creative process? — I'm most inspired by things I see around me. I remember doing a drawing I called the Lewisham Girl: It was a picture of a girl I spotted on the street who was wearing a kilt, and I thought she looked great. I'm also inspired by photographs in old social history books and by film stars, such as Katharine Hepburn's style in trousers or women like Amy Johnson, the pilot; I was often inspired by modern independent women in this new world of equality with men, wearing the trousers. In terms of men's clothing (which I started out with) it was all about softening and relaxing the shirt. I loved the quality of shirts, but I didn't love the shirts that you'd get in Jermyn Street with those stiff collars. I think that's what men responded to: the relaxed quality of the make and fabric, and the little details that made it feel different.

What makes a design timeless? — Well-designed products tend to endure. They become our classics, like the Anglepoise light or Braun clocks. It's important that pieces consider form, function and being made with the right materials for the job.

How many different artisan communities do you currently work with? — I work with quite a few. There's Mackintosh, who make the rubberized raincoats that I love so much and are still a bestseller after all these years. We also work with a half-dozen small Scottish knitwear companies, many on the borders in Hawick. Then there is Whitehouse Cox, who started off as saddle makers, whose leatherwork we use on bags and belts, and we also work with London Tradition for duffle coats and Tricker's for shoes.

Many of these are generations-old companies. What are the biggest challenges they face? — Many older companies could benefit from doing more to attract young people to learn the trade. Some companies in Scotland are housed in very old Victorian buildings and others have renovated newer factories to make them more efficient and attractive to work in. One of the biggest challenges they face is trying to get younger employees in. If they were offering the

right pay and the right conditions, I think many young people would enjoy being taught these crafts and would get the same satisfaction and pride that older people have with their work. The older generation needs to pass on these skills, but they also need to stay updated.

How do you create products that delicately balance modern innovation with being rooted in tradition? — I think it's all to do with the choice of fabric: the lightness, the construction, the cut, the color. Color is quite far down the list, but it's still important. These days it's difficult to use Harris tweeds in those lovely natural colors because it feels a bit too country, whereas in black or dark gray, they're still delicious.

How have your design values changed over time? — I used to love going into charity shops, but they're now so stuffed with clothes that I don't enjoy it as much. That's the result of chain stores selling cheap products from China and people being seduced into buying far more than they need. I'm sure that leads to a lack of good values in terms of respecting and looking after things, which were the post-war values my parents raised me with. You really don't need masses of things when perhaps one or two things will do—I'll always prefer having one thing that cost more money but is something I really like and will live with for a long time.

Why is it important to make consumers aware of the stories behind products and to tell them where these pieces have come from? — Sometimes people have no idea how much really goes into production—how many hands and processes it goes through—so we made a series of brochures showing our products being made. I think it's important that the consumers are aware of this and that these stories explain the value of the products.

How can design help the cultivation of local communities? — I think design in general—our street design, our buildings,

our schools—can have a big influence on community. Design can also help communities. For example, the Maggie's Centres are drop-in centers for cancer patients across the UK: They've brought in well-known designers to build these beautiful spaces with lovely gardens, and they've found it really does make a difference. Another example is the Royal Festival Hall in London: It was built for the 1951 Festival of Britain to uplift the people's spirits. The building itself is timeless and has lasted because it's beautifully designed and they put value on the materials used. It's still a thriving community building.

How do timely consumer trends influence product design? — Trends can be exciting, but I don't think that way; trend-based thinking doesn't affect me. I create in the present, and I'd never profess to know what the future will be! But I might have thoughts back to the past. The way I work is more a response to seeing something and interpreting it; it's a very intuitive response. I don't really think of what I do as fashion—I see it as designing clothes that have the right feel for that day or for that particular lifestyle. Everything I do stems from a lifestyle approach.

It's not just about clothes: Your stores are also filled with kitchenware and furniture in addition to British design exhibitions. How did this evolution come about? — When we moved to Wigmore Street in 2002, I'd been designing clothes for 30 years. I thought it'd be an opportunity to create a nice setting for the clothes by putting things I liked around them—the same aesthetic but in different forms. So I decided to create the challenge of putting on small exhibitions of other British designers who interested me. The Wigmore Street shop space is very long, like a gallery, so it worked very well. It was simply a case of increasing and diversifying what we were already doing in a very natural way. It's about creating an entire lifestyle, and it's also a good way to bring like-minded people together. DD

Petra Olsson Gendt & Tanja Vibe, All the Way to Paris

The friends behind this Copenhagen-based design studio discuss positive cooperation and how every idea is worth putting up on the wall.

When Petra Olsson Gendt calls from her home in Malmö, Sweden, the graphic designer is in the midst of preparing dinner for 18: cabbage, peaches with buffalo mozzarella and grilled fresh sausages. Petra and her business partner, Tanja Vibe, are used to multitasking though: As founders of the Copenhagen design firm All the Way to Paris (ATWTP), they and their team of six designers and art directors collaborate with a wide array of chefs, artists and heritage furniture brands all while maintaining their signature playful and clean aesthetic. ATWTP does everything from designing ink blot-inspired tea logos to working on wrapping paper for HAY or creating cookie cutters for Georg Jensen. Their projects all fall under what they call "conceptual communication:" an intuitive form of visual branding that helps convey the ethos of a company through its look, feel and immediate impact. We spoke with them about collaboration, communication and the importance of standing your ground.

When did you two start working together? — *Tanja (left):* We met at the Royal Danish Academy of Fine Arts where we were studying graphic design. We started working together almost immediately as we had a similar aesthetic and the same goals. People come to school with different aims, and we were both focused on our work rather than, you know, being focused on having beers! We found each other and that became our community both socially and in a design sense—we've always worked well together and have also gotten along very well personally. So in 2004, we decided to start All the Way to Paris.

After working so closely with each other for so long, is it hard to balance your personal and professional lives? — *Petra (right):* Tanja and I have a very whole relationship—it's both super professional and personal; we can't separate them. We know each other very well, so luckily our husbands and six kids get along—we've been on several vacations together and love to travel.

What do you both bring to your partnership? — *Petra:* Tanja is very, very good at design. She has a strong feeling for colors, and when she starts sketching, she produces work quickly and it's always interesting. I'm slower and maybe more critical—that makes me sound very boring! But we balance each other out. Sometimes we'll come out of a meeting and Tanja will say, "That was great!" and I'll say, "Actually, that wasn't great at all!" She's very positive—I think it's quite a Danish quality. I'm Swedish, and I think there's something of the Swedish melancholy and deliberateness in me, while she's very happy-go-lucky. So we're a good team.

How do you describe the aesthetic you share? — *Petra:* I'd say that ATWTP has a classic and raw aesthetic—minimalism, but still with tension. Tanja has a raw sense

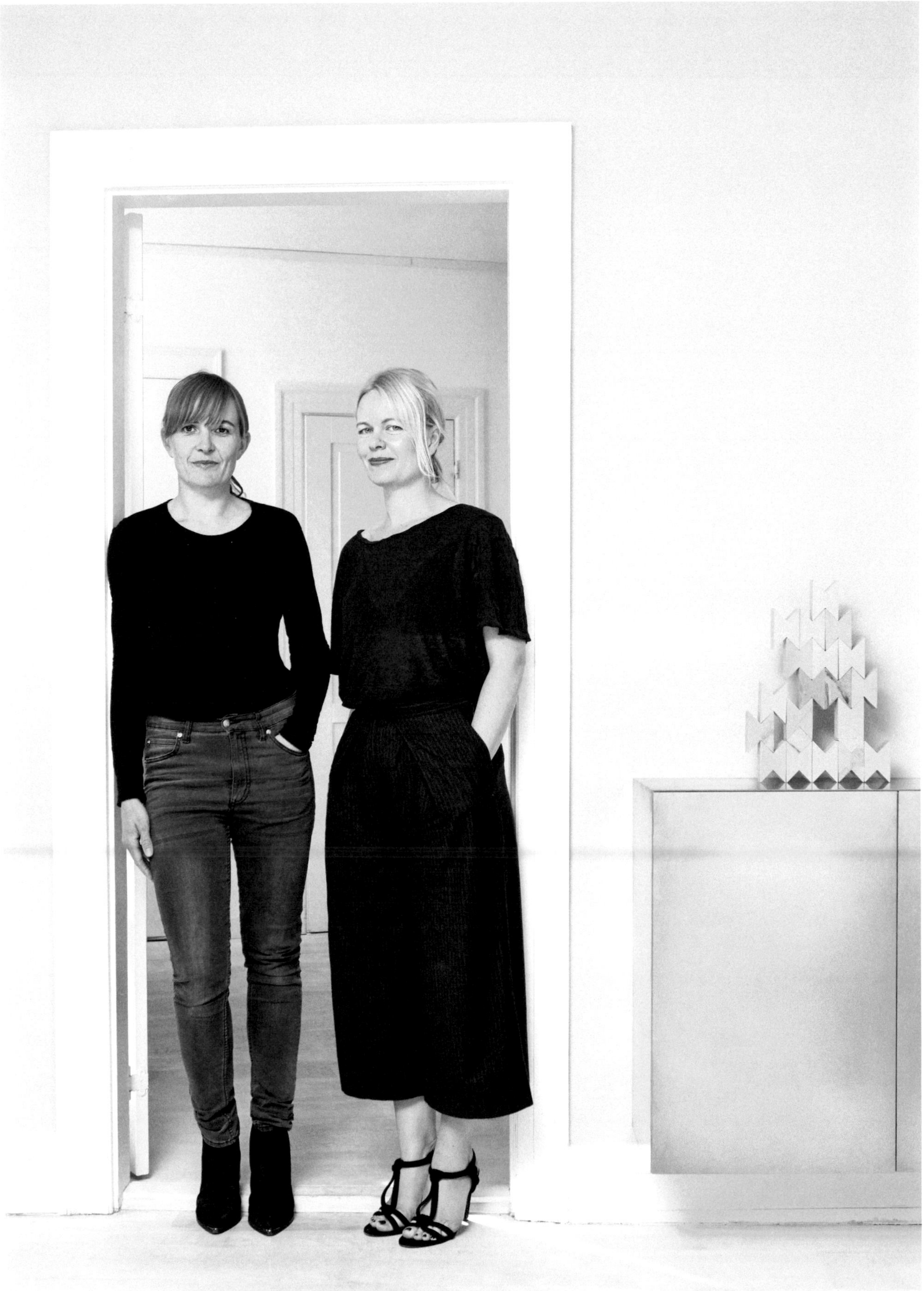

PHOTOGRAPH: CHRISTIAN FRIIS

Above: Sketches and photos speckle the walls of All the Way to Paris's Copenhagen studio. Founders Petra Olsson Gendt and Tanja Vibe believe that any idea—no matter how big or small—should have its time on the wall to be considered.

> "Dialogue is really important, and we love it when a client challenges us—when they know what they want, and we know what we want."

of the contemporary—she works with simple aesthetics and can make magic with small means. My approach to projects is often from the communicative angle: I'll ask myself, "How does this style or this choice of type communicate the content and the message?"

How involved are you with the Copenhagen design community? — *Tanja:* It's a very vibrant community. Scandinavia put the spotlight on style early on. There's a tradition there, but we also question and happily propose new styles and design at the same time. Petra and I are definitely a part of it: We both teach, are on design juries and are very social people. But it's so easy to get too caught up in socializing or uniformity. I think Scandinavian design is very homogeneous, so we try our best to not *only* be Scandinavian. Staying focused on our own projects is key, and we're *extremely* focused on what we do and on our clients—the dialogue with them consumes us. We're lucky that we usually have long-term clients, and they become our community.

How does teaching impact your process? — *Tanja:* Students are curious, ambitious and want to explore and learn to get better. The students and the educational environment remind you of why you are working with this world in the first place. This feeling or dynamic is something we try very hard to keep at the office. With any client or anyone on the team, we want to ask *why are you here?* rather than *what do you do here?*

What attracts you to a particular project? — *Petra:* In the beginning, we couldn't afford to be so picky—we took all kinds of projects just to feed ourselves. But you learn from all of those experiences, and I really believe that if you do good work, you get good work. That's something I always tell my design students. When we were first starting out, we were fortunate to have a network of friends in the design world, and we really benefited from good word-of-mouth. We're very lucky now that we can choose our clients and that people

know our work and know us personally, so we don't really need to sell ourselves. The collaborations need to work for everyone though; whoever the client is, we need to have the same approach. This includes aesthetically, but anything that attracts us also needs to have content. There has to be something there, and we definitely look for sympathetic people. We have big commercial clients, but they're commercial clients with passion! Whoever they are, they need to be doing something passionately.

What kind of diplomacy is required when working with clients' ideas and your own vision? — *Tanja:* We're quite open—extremely open, in fact—to hearing other points of view. Dialogue is really important, and we love it when a client challenges us—when they know what they want, and we know what we want. In fact, we don't want a client who agrees with everything at this point in our careers. Sometimes we'll look at each other and say, "That was too easy!" We work with one Danish furniture maker who really pushes us and actually uses the words, "I'm going to challenge you on that—I think you can take it further." And we love that! It's what keeps it interesting.

What's your collaborative process like? — *Petra:* That first meeting is where we just listen to a client and what they want. Then we go back to the office and brainstorm with our team of graphic designers. We sketch, we put ideas up on the walls, and we always tell people to put *everything* up on the wall, even if it's an idea they're not sure of. Ultimately, we narrow it down to two or three approaches, as more than that is confusing. We don't try to present something that's ready; we like to involve the client at quite an early stage. There can be a pureness, a rawness in an undeveloped idea—an idea that can't fully carry the message or isn't strong enough aesthetically but has something to build on and develop. I guess it all comes down to working hard with all the possibilities and then being good at choosing: Sometimes you have to be willing to kill your darlings. SS

Natasha Jen, Pentagram

Over the past 15 years, this Taiwan-born, New York-based graphic designer has come a complete, digitally rendered circle from aspiring intern to inspiring leader.

Not even Natasha Jen can quite fathom the enviable position she's worked so hard to achieve. Born in Taipei, Taiwan, Natasha originally moved to New York to study painting, but her mother asked her to consider switching majors to something that one day might get her a "real job." This led her toward the graphic design department on a whim, and shortly after, she landed an interning stint at legendary design firm Pentagram. After spending the next 11 years working in different studios and with her own creative practice, in 2012 she was asked back to the very firm where she first got her foot in the door—this time, as a partner. Now as one of the youngest-ever partners at Pentagram, Natasha works with a diverse collection of clients ranging from the Metropolitan Museum of Art to Apex, a mentoring program for disadvantaged Asian and immigrant youth in New York. She talks to us about setting your own personal expectations while partaking in the jam session of teamwork.

Please tell us more about Pentagram. How do their leadership teams operate, and what are the advantages of having a lateral chain of command? — Pentagram is a culture, a place and a business that celebrates differences. Extreme differences. It's owned and managed by a team of partners, and each partner has a different design philosophy, an autonomous team and does very different projects. As a partner, you define your own goals on your own terms, and your fellow partners are there to support your goals. There's a tremendous amount of freedom that's similar to a mom-and-pop shop, yet it provides the platform and support to do large-scale work. Pentagram is small compared to many branding agencies, but because we are small, we interact with our teams, partners and clients more intimately and directly. There is less bureaucracy than you would find in a typical corporate culture. You can't find a business model more utopian than this!

You started at Pentagram as an intern over a decade before you were asked back to be one of their youngest-ever creative partners: How have you learned to get people to take you seriously and respect your work? — I don't really contemplate how I'm perceived or whether I've lived up to other people's measurements of success. When I was asked on as a partner in 2012, there was a lot of self-doubt and anxiety that came along with it. So over the last few years, my main goal has been to build my team and our own body of work. I think graphic design produces work that's social by nature: The work is meant to be seen, experienced and used by groups of people. Of course it feels good when people resonate with what we do at Pentagram, but if not, that's okay! Looking back, we've done a tremendous amount of work that's far beyond what I initially projected we'd do, but the fact is that we're still at the very beginning stage of a practice and we have a lot to explore and accomplish. I'm still at a start-up stage in life. The creative anxiety remains, but now it's a healthier, self-motivated one.

Above: Though design firm Pentagram has offices all over the world, Natasha Jen calls their New York location home. Born and raised in Taipei where neon signs and vibrant colors abound, she says her Taiwanese upbringing brings a sense of humor and playfulness to her work.

> "Graphic design produces work that's social by nature: The work is meant to be seen, experienced and used by groups of people."

What have you learned about teamwork both through working for large organizations and running your own small studio? — Teamwork can seem like a symphony orchestra, but in reality it's more like a jazz band: You can't always predict how people perform, so you have to improvise and be okay with that.

How have you learned when to break the rules and when to follow them? — Growing up, I wouldn't say that I was rebellious, but I was pretty independent. For example, while other kids were taken to school by their parents, I took a one-hour public bus ride to school by myself starting when I was 6 years old. My mom couldn't have been more proud of me, then or now. I actually enjoyed being on a crowded bus with strangers and adults because they'd always give me a seat! I'm rarely bothered by rules: If I find rules unreasonable, I just walk away from them. I mean, why bang your head against someone else's systems? We have the freedom to choose our own comfort zones.

What elements of your Taiwanese upbringing have you brought to New York? — To be able to see humor in everything—that's a big Taiwanese cultural trait. The second thing is my infinite interest in food. Taiwan has an incredible food culture and philosophy: Eat often, eat well, eat everything. I have lived by that principle wherever I go.

What have you learned about the realities of trying to maintain a work/life balance? — Graphic design is a creative business as well as a service business. The combination of the two can be deadly chaotic. It takes a lot of trial and error and a good amount of intuition to figure out the fabric of things and, most importantly, learning when to say no. There's no formula to that—you just have to test things constantly and find an answer for yourself. I think I'm still in that testing mode.

How do you switch off from work at the end of the day? — I've been traveling to different time zones a lot over the past two years, so instead of having a clear starting and ending point, now I feel that I use my time more and more fluidly. Because I don't have a regimented sleeping pattern like I used to, I have to be more spontaneous about off-work activities. I read, I wander aimlessly on streets and I discover things—it's pretty fun.

Where do good ideas come from? — Dissatisfaction or boredom.

How can we stay original when we are so saturated by other people's work? — I think originality is a lofty goal; I'd prefer "betterment." The reality of the digital age is that it's impossible to escape from information unless we decide to live off the grid. Everything can be easily compared to something else from the present and past, and we're constantly bombarded with those comparisons. It's like living in a giant blender!

Are you an endless perfectionist? How do you know when a design is "done" and move on from it? — I'm a pragmatic precisionist: I prefer precision over perfection. Perfection is hard to define, but precision (or the lack of it) is tangible. In order to be precise about design, there's the whole backend that needs to be configured first—finding the right people, assigning them the right tasks and setting the right expectations—that is as important as the designing itself.

Do you believe there is power in doing one thing and doing it well, or is there greater power in being a generalist? — I believe that doing what you're truly passionate about drives excellence, whether it's a single focus or a broader take on things. Only passion can motivate tired practice.

What is your overarching philosophy when it comes to what constitutes good design? — It's design that opens up new ways to see the same old things, has thoughtful details and doesn't break—it's easy to say, hard to do. GFK

Karl Fournier & Olivier Marty, Studio KO

Although these French architects' large-scale projects have taken them across multiple continents, they still maintain their studio's esprit de corps.

With offices split across Paris, London and Marrakech, Studio KO's architectural style encompasses stark simplicity and quirky opulence. By fusing their traditional design backgrounds with Moroccan influences, Karl Fournier and Olivier Marty create vibrant interior and exterior experiences with an abundance of warmth and a dash of eccentricity. They work across everything from "abstraction to architecture" and devise both private and public spaces for clients throughout Europe, Northern Africa and the Americas. They speak to us about how everything they do is influenced by partnership: between cities, between styles, between clients and between each other.

What is your view on longevity in design? — *Karl (right):* We think that following our path without trying to foresee the future will make our designs durable in the decades to come.

How have you learned to balance a client's wants and needs with maintaining your own creative edge? — *Olivier (left):* We often say that a great idea is not the average of everyone's good ideas. On the other hand, projects involving the owners' suggestions and considerations are often the best ones. We always start by forming a strong conceptual statement for each project and constantly refer back to it.

How is it different designing for a private individual (for a home or apartment) versus designing for public audiences (for boutiques and hotels)? — *Karl:* Private residential projects have a major ingredient that enriches the process: the client—their obsessions, taboos, fears and dreams. When it comes to public projects where we don't necessarily know the audience, we often create a narrative that envisions a specific story for characters within the space. That helps us make the project alive and vibrant.

What are some design tricks that encourage us to interact with one another? — *Olivier:* People from different backgrounds share architectural objects around them, and they experience them from different perspectives. It's amazing to notice how a room can suddenly become full of friends just because you added soft pillows, or how there's always an exciting energy where the drinks are located at a party.

How important is it to retain the history of the space you're working with? Why? —*Karl:* When we work on existing buildings, we always start from the "bones" of the building. We feel that this process of archeology is essential: We put the rip-out on hold until we have surveyed all the little details that define the architectural language.

Above: Nestled in the Atlas Mountains near Marrakech, the clay-covered walls and clean lines of Studio KO's Villa K pay tribute to both historical and contemporary design. With offices in Paris, London and Morocco, partners Karl Fournier and Olivier Marty spend a lot of time exploring this exotic location.

"There is a constant support that comes from love—it makes the duet much stronger than solely being business partners."

What is your relationship with the natural world when you are designing constructs within it? — *Olivier:* For the Villa E [one of a series of lodges built in the foothills of the Atlas Mountains in Morocco], we focused on the solar orientation and the relationship with its location. We used mainly local resources such as stone that was directly extracted from the soil. It probably explains how immediate and natural the house now looks in its beautiful surroundings.

Your designs often mix opulent and quirky elements with stark simplicity. What is the key to achieving the perfect balance of both? — *Karl:* We choose an object for the power it has and its significance. Not, "Ah, it's pretty—the color will match well..."

How are your personalities portrayed through the work you do? — *Olivier:* We use a wide range of languages for our projects. But what remains constant is the attitude, which is what defines us. There are also probably some major elements of our personalities that appear in the architecture; sincerity could be one of them.

Why did you decide to open an office in Marrakech? How has this choice influenced the aesthetic of your work? — *Olivier:* It happened by chance through an amazing French Moroccan—we started off as clients, and we then became close friends. A few years or so after that, we were offered our first commission there, and it all happened very quickly. We built an incredible network in Morocco: Hermès, Agnelli, Saint Laurent and Pierre Bergé. But above all, it allowed us to discover the strength of the local craftsmanship and gave us the desire to emphasize that craft as a key element of our work. There is a much stronger common root between Eastern and Western design than what you would expect. Gradually, some professional relationships have even turned into friendships.

What have you learned from your time spent in Marrakech that you have applied to your personal life? — *Olivier:* In Marrakech, there's a different approach to time and a certain distance that makes you realize that there's a solution for everything.

How important is a sense of humor in your line of work? — *Karl:* It's compulsory! Even if it's hard, we should never take ourselves too seriously—starting with the atmosphere at the office. We have a project to collect all the jokes that our staff make while working.

What are the advantages of working with your partner? — *Karl:* There is a constant support that comes from love—it makes the duet much stronger than solely being business partners. Satisfaction and reward come at the same moment. Sharing the creation of architectural objects inspires a very strong feeling, almost like having children—however, that will not prevent us from also having kids of our own one day!

How have you learned where to push and pull depending on each other's talents? — *Olivier:* It's a complex issue that's never completely solved. It moves—like a living body—and the moments when both of us are equally sharing involvement and creativity are precious. GFK

WORDS
ADRIENNE MATEI

PHOTOGRAPHS
MAIA FLORE

Neighborhood: Libraries

Public libraries speak volumes about our communities. From the Ancient Greeks' ornate marble displays through to the digital era's shifting designs, these shared spaces provide whole neighborhoods with a location to share ideas as well as knowledge (as long as you keep respectfully quiet).

Straddling the US and Canadian border, the Haskell Free Library and Opera House has a black stripe across its floor that separates Vermont and Quebec. The 110-year-old library is a designated heritage site for the two countries—a symbol of shared culture and community. To border patrol, it's a headache, but to the locals who visit Haskell, their public library is a place to read, socialize and take in cultural performances with their neighbors—even if the stage is technically in Canada and the seats are in the States. During an era when the public library's staying power is diminishing, Haskell is a reminder that these spaces have existed for millennia as physical manifestations of equality, knowledge and community—unbiased areas that encourage neighbors of all types (even nations, in this case) to come and learn in one mutual environment.

Public libraries exude an ancient quality that makes them seem like they've always been there. Like Tolkien's wizards, libraries appear so eternally wise that it's almost impossible to imagine them in any kind of undignified infancy. After all, humanity has been collecting texts to demonstrate and develop an understanding of the world since the creation of the written word.

However, until relatively recently, access to these texts had been exclusively restricted to certain members of society. More than 2,250 years ago, only scholars, royals and rich bibliophiles were welcome in Ancient Egypt's Library of Alexandria, which boasted a massive inventory of texts categorized via systems developed by Aristotle. As Ancient Egyptians believed that writing was a way of communicating with the future, scribes also enjoyed special library privileges along with an elevated social status. The role of gifted writers was to create textual time capsules in the hope that their civilization's accomplishments would always be remembered. And in some ways, they were right, for now many of their tomes sit beside each other in the very establishments in which they once penned (or quilled) those histories.

The first public libraries opened in Rome shortly after the Library of Alexandria was destroyed during the Roman conquest of Egypt in 30 B.C.—Caesar saw its loss as an opportunity to establish Rome as the epicenter of intellectualism. And how better to one-up a civilization than by encouraging the dissemination of impressive academia, effectively creating a more enlightened populace? In a society that equated books with prestige, Roman scholars who were unable to afford the lavish personal libraries that were trendy among the wealthy had now been granted a means to learn.

The intellectuals of the time also believed that a library's architecture should reflect the empowerment of society. As a result, these buildings were built to communicate the breadth of knowledge that the people had at their disposal, complete with dramatic entry staircases that conveyed a sense of astral ascendance toward education. Likewise, cultural rulers began to scoff

These photographs were taken at the Stuttgart Municipal Library in Germany. The monolithic structure is nine stories tall and is accessible from all four sides. Also referred to as "The Cube" by locals, the design centers around primary shapes, plain surfaces and the purity of form.

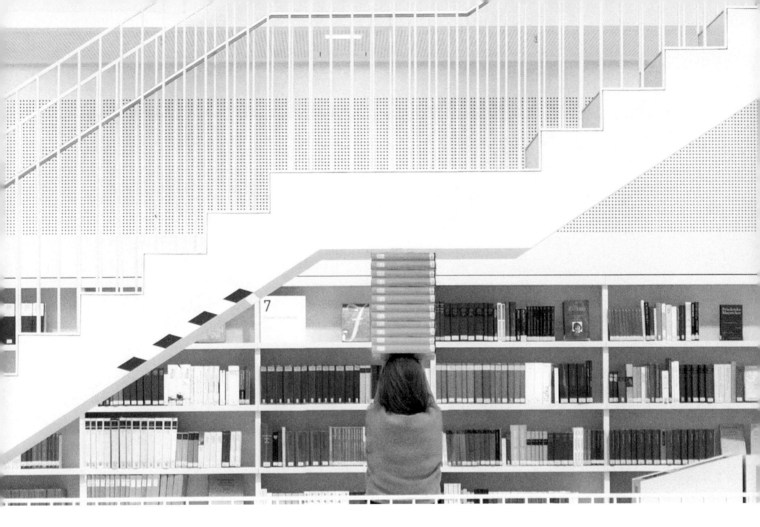

at the misappropriation of books as home decor. Roman playwright Seneca eye-rolled at private libraries in *De Tranquillitate Animi*, writing that personal book collections were too often assembled for show as home decor rather than serving their true purpose of being spread and read.

Though it may seem like an odd match today, many of Rome's public libraries were built as additions to public bathhouses. These institutions were said to be lavish and well-respected community centers where all levels of society congregated to chat, soak, eat and—for the literate minority—read.

Following the fall of the Roman Empire in the fifth century, the intellectual Dark Ages caused the general public's literacy rates to dip even lower than their already dismal levels. During this time, libraries were kept alive by monastic communities such as the Byzantine monks, who believed reading and writing were essential for spiritual development. They customarily loaned their sacred works to neighboring

monasteries, thereby technically creating the world's first inter-library loan (no word on late fees).

The Renaissance of the 14th century saw a resurgence of Greco-Roman educational ideals. Private book collections were still the domains of the wealthy, but public libraries surged in popularity particularly after the 15th-century invention of the printing press made literature easier to circulate. Through both technological and cultural evolutions such as these, libraries have supported intellectual freedom, free speech and creative property through the ages. And above all, they have championed social equality by making resources increasingly more accessible to everyone.

Regardless of geographic location, libraries are uniquely situated between the private and public realms. Unlike bookstores, libraries are free from consumerist expectations: There's no purchase necessary to spend an entire rainy afternoon harvesting new reads, and all walks of life

are welcome, as long as they respond compliantly to a pointed "shhh". They uniquely toe the line between lounge room and town square, which leads to all kinds of small territorial acquisitions—the full-day carrel stake-out, the tabletop stationery sprawl—as well as the inevitable surprises that occur when diverse groups of strangers share a space, such as stumbling upon someone napping between the stacks or brushing their teeth in the bathroom. We can be privately absorbed in a novel that bears the decades-old underlined passages and dog-eared pages of those who've come before us, all the while being present in the sphere of public life.

As modern methods of gathering information have evolved, so has our practical use of the library. For many, internet searches have replaced card catalogs, but libraries still offer active experiences that no passive content provider can replicate.

A new technology movement aims to provide public library patrons with even

Designed by Cologne-based Yi Architects
and built in 2011, Stuttgart's Municipal Library
is built around a four-story contemplation
chamber that is surrounded by study rooms.
Other areas include the reading room, which is
encased by white staircases and a skylit ceiling,
a cafeteria and a seminar space.

more opportunities for activity and inter-action. More than 2,000 workshops called Makerspaces (or Fab Labs) have opened in various places—including many public libraries—worldwide, allowing visitors the chance to not only accumulate knowledge, but to apply it. "Makerspaces are creative, DIY spaces where people can gather to in-vent and learn," explains Jeroen de Boer, whose work with FryskLab, a Makerspace at the Library Service Friesland, earned him a nomination for the Netherlands' 2015 Librarian of the Year. Makerspaces encour-age new inventions that can be made for the price of a library card with tools that would otherwise be expensive and inaccessible. His co-authored 2015 book, *Makerspaces in Libraries*, expands on how these facilities are "bringing back the value of making things yourself and with others" by acting as labo-ratories where library patrons can actualize their own creative designs using relatively low-cost hardware and software (as well as information from books and the web).

"Libraries have always been places for gaining knowledge, building insight and launching investigations into the nature of things," de Boer says. "The whole idea of a Makerspace is to make tools and knowl-edge available to everyone."

And it's not just the technology within libraries that has advanced—their physical entities have adapted too, and the forms libraries have now taken are endless. You'll find a library within a repurposed army tank in Buenos Aires, roadside in a small New Zealand town and open-air in a Tel Aviv park. The Liyuan Library on the outskirts of Beijing employs the twigs that locals use for firewood as a building material, the Taipei Public Library is the country's most eco-conscious building (it collects rainwater and uses photovoltaic solar power) and the Picture Book Library in Iwaki, Japan, skips a spine-out approach in favor of displaying every book cover face-forward to create a rainbow honeycomb of tantalizingly visi-ble stories. Each distinct library conveys

a narrative of its community's identity, both present and past.

What we read becomes part of us. Libraries facilitate discoveries, introduce us to untold facts and propel us into the minds of characters. They contextualize our lives in a greater scheme and help us find rea-sons to relate to each other. Every balance from the atmospheric mix of cozy and vast spaces to the social cocktail of public life and satisfying introversion has played a part in the spread of knowledge and develop-ment of civilization as we know it.

Most importantly, libraries are capa-ble of inspiring imagination and a sense of intellectual adventure. They emanate a seductive pull that should not be under-estimated—the mesmerizing promise of row upon row of beckoning, beautiful books. Libraries are more than the sum of their parts or the books in their catalogs: They also serve as entry points into the infinite adventures waiting to be selected from their shelves and enacted together.

ISSUE EIGHTEEN CREDITS

SPECIAL THANKS
Thanks to Katrin Coetzer for the Starters and Design illustrations

ON THE COVER
Photographer Pelle Crépin
Photographer's Assistant Joseph Seresin
Photographer's Assistant Bruno Baptista
Styling Ruth Higginbotham
Hair Paul Donovan at CLM using Bumble and Bumble
Makeup Linda Andersson
Model Vanessa at Elite London
Casting Sarah Bunter
Production We Are Up Production
Special thanks to Thomas Howard

Clothing Top and skirt by Joseph

HAPPINESS BY DESIGN
Photographer Daniel Schriver
Styling Sara Ingemann at Atelier Cph
Art Direction Mandy Rep at Atelier Cph
Hair and Makeup Louise Thydal
Model Julie Beider at Le Management
Special thanks to Sonja Lyubomirsky

Ceramics Can by Casalinga; bowl and glass bottle by Menu; cup by HAY; round bowl by Studio Arhoj; glass by Notre Dame

SENSE IN SYMMETRY
Photographer Daniel Schriver
Styling Sara Ingemann at Atelier Cph
Art Direction Mandy Rep at Atelier Cph

Ceramics Diamond by Bloomingville; round box by Bolia; candle holder by Menu; wooden shapes by HAY

THE WHY OF THE STORM
Illustrator Katrin Coetzer

THE NATURE OF DESIRABILITY
Photographer Daniel Schriver
Styling Sara Ingemann at Atelier Cph
Art Direction Mandy Rep at Atelier Cph

Ceramics Wooden items and cork cone by HAY; bottle by Menu; vase by Bolia; boxes by ferm LIVING

THE LUNCH BOX: GEOMETRIC SNACKS
Photographer Anders Schønnemann
Food Styling Mikkel Karstad
Prop Styling Sidsel Rudolph

NIKOLAJ & MATHIAS MENTZE
Photographer Christian Friis

KAI AVENT-DELEON
Photographer Zoltan Tombor
Special thanks to Sarah Lalenya Kazalski at See Management

MAX LAMB
Photographer Phil Dunlop

A VIEW FROM THE PORCH
From the book A View From the Porch *by Avi Friedman. Copyright 2015. Reprinted with permission of Véhicule Press*
Photographer Anders Schønnemann
Special thanks to Isis-Colombe Combréas, Karel Balas, Simon Dardick, Maya Assouad and Julie Boucherat

IN CONVERSATION: ISLE CRAWFORD & HUGO MACDONALD
Special thanks to Christopher Beanland, Morgwn Rimel and the team at The School of Life

COMPARE AND CONTRAST
Photographer Pelle Crépin
Photographer's Assistant Joseph Seresin
Photographer's Assistant Bruno Baptista
Styling Ruth Higginbotham
Hair Paul Donovan at CLM using
Bumble and Bumble
Makeup Linda Andersson
Models Stephan and Yan at PRM, Alys
and Alex at IMG, Vanessa at Elite London
and Phillip at Nevs
Casting Sarah Bunter
Production We Are Up Production
Special thanks to Thomas Howard

Clothing
Page 59: Sweater by Joseph
Page 60: Sweater by Proenza Schouler
at Net-A-Porter*; turtleneck by Uniqlo
Page 61: T-shirt by James Perse at
Mr Porter*; shirt by Timothy Everest
Page 62: Sweater by Proenza Schouler
at Net-A-Porter
Page 63: Sweater by Jil Sander
Page 64: Shirt and sweater* by Z Zegna
Page 65: Sweater by Joseph
Page 66: Dress by Acne Studios*
Page 67: Sweater by Joseph
Page 68: Sweater and trousers by Paul Smith
Page 69: Shirt by Z Zegna; skirt by Joseph
* *The colors of these items have been altered*
for this editorial

A DAY IN THE LIFE:
NEW TENDENCY
Photographer Anders Schønnemann
Locations Agnes Cafeteria, Chipperfield
Kantine, Galerie Johann König St.Agnes,
Nathanja & Heinrich, New Tendency
Studio and Weydinger Strasse
Special thanks to Lilli Heinemann

CONNECTING THE LOTS
Photographer Justin Fantl
Special thanks to Rachel Goldman
at Giant Artists

NATURAL PERSPECTIVE:
MICHELE OKA DONER
Photographer Matthew Sprout
Hair Elin Nyberg
Makeup Deanna Hagen at Kate Ryan
Agency

ORDER IN THE COURTS
Photographer Neil Bedford
Styling Camilla Pole
Hair Mirka Hajdova at Saint Luke using
Bumble and Bumble
Makeup Crystabel Riley at Stella Creative
Models Kesse at Premier and Tessa at
Wilhelmina
Casting Sarah Bunter
Retouching Oliver Carver
Production We Are Up Production
Special thanks to Thomas Howard

Clothing
Page 107: His polo by Fred Perry; shorts by
Nike; sneakers by Puma; socks are stylist's
own. Her sweater by Acne Studios; skirt by
American Apparel; sneakers by Nike; socks
are stylist's own
Page 109: Top and skirt by American
Apparel
Page 110: Crop top by Orlebar Brown;
shorts by American Apparel; socks and
sneakers by Adidas
Page 111: T-shirt and shorts by Todd Snyder
Page 113: Pants and jacket by Le Coq
Sportif
Page 114: T-shirt and shorts by Todd
Snyder; socks by Wilson; sneakers by Adidas
Page 117: Turtleneck by Uniqlo; sweater
by Sunspel; pants by Acne Studios; sneakers
by Converse

THE BLACK & WHITE MENU
Photographer Anders Schønnemann
Food Styling Mikkel Karstad
Prop Styling Sidsel Rudolph

Ceramics Items on page 122–123 by
Sidsel Rudolph; all other items by
Gurli Elbækgaard

PROFILE SERIES:
SNARKITECTURE
Photographer Nicole Franzen
Special thanks to Olivia Colson

PROFILE SERIES:
MARGARET HOWELL
Photographer Phil Dunlop
Special thanks to Kerry Francis

PROFILE SERIES:
ALL THE WAY TO PARIS
Photographer Christian Friis

PROFILE SERIES:
NATASHA JEN
Photographer Zoltan Tombor
Styling Soukéna Roussi
Special thanks to Stephanie Land and
Sarah Lalenya Kazalski at See Management

Clothing
Dress by Titania Inglis

PROFILE SERIES:
STUDIO KO
Portrait Photographer Noel Manalili
Architecture Photographer Dan Glasser
Special thanks to Sofia Di Leva

NEIGHBORHOOD:
LIBRARIES
Location Stuttgart Municipal Library,
Stuttgart, Germany